# INFLAMMAGING

## UNLOCKING THE SECRETS TO

## INFLAMMATION AND AGING

By

Dr. Mark Luckie

Foreword by Dr. Mark S. Miller

# DEDICATION

For my children Hannah, Foster, Hudson, and Isla-
whom I hope live well into their years without
the hardships of the aging process. And that I am
blessed to see each step.

# FOREWARD by Dr. Mark S Miller

Health is a state of balance. A state where all the checks and balances are in place and operating effectively. By contrast, illness or poor health is typified by a challenge or disturbance to this state of balance. A situation where one or several systems are either diminished or excessive, or both. As Dr. Luckie explains the ultimate goal of any wellness orientation intervention is to restore balance and harmony, thereby maintaining form and function.

In this delightful book, Dr. Mark Luckie outlines some of the common challenges to our health and wellness. Forces that disturb this state of balance and ultimately compromise our well-being. From this intimate knowledge of the critical biomedical players in these events, one candesign targeted and effective solutions. Understanding the problems in detail is the critical first step in regaining health.

What is so helpful in this book is that Dr. Luckie not only guides us through the problem-solution interface, but he does this in a beautifully lay-friendly style. Not an easy task. It is accessible, understandable, relatable and effective. Armed with this information one is extricated from the fog of not knowing what to do, and placed in a vista of clarity, where you can make better decisions. Choices that are targeted at the problem at hand. Understand and define the problem and then plug in a solution, all done in a manner that everyone can understand.

Those that know Dr. Luckie appreciates how passionate he is in bringing wellness to the masses.This goes well beyond the people that he sees in his clinic or having just met. His passion extends to everyone. This book represents another stepping-stone in his servant journey. A Journey that will be remarkably rewarding, both for him and for the recipients. I am delighted to have the opportunity to bring this book to your attention. I encourage you to savor the wisdom, put the knowledge and lessons into practice. Follow his guidance and I am truly confident that you will be in a healthier place.

# Mark JS Miller

Email: markjsm03@gmail.com
https://drmarkjsmiller.substack.com/

CIO/CSO/VP/President

# PROFESSIONAL SUMMARY

An internationally recognized elite biomedical researcher, entrepreneur, product development innovator, marketing and brand developer, regulatory executive with a history of success in academic medicine, as well cross platform business channels in health, wellness, dietary supplements and functional foods. Innovation and process management to execute a competitive edge are critical skills. Highly skilled in teamwork, creative problem solving and top level functioning in fast paced, challenging environments. A recognized Key Opinion Leader within the natural product and biotechnology industries.

- C-suite leadership team member (Chief Innovation Officer) of a Private Investment group within the contract manufacturing sector of the natural products industry

- Board member within the Contract Manufacturing space for nutritionals after a successful M&A
- Chief Innovation Officer for a Beauty from Within company in a hybrid business model focusing on Influencer Marketing. Responsible for product development, intellectual property, manufacturing and consumer education
- Innovator & Serial Disruptor in product development, marketing, consumer education and biomedical research.
- Medical School Professor in three USA medical schools (tenured Full Professor in my '30's)
- Drug Discovery Director in a major Swiss pharmaceutical company
- As CSO increased Sales From $73M to $665M in 6 Years in a direct sales company
- For a Network Marketing company raised "diamond level" distributorships from 7 to 123 in 6 years
- Disruption of the joint health sector of the natural products industry
- Company spokesperson, brand-builder and voice of credibility & trust
- Research discoveries have fundamentally changed how we view and treat disease in numerous medical disciplines.

# Preface

I was inspired and challenged to write my first book by one of my mentors, Grant Cardone during the course of my attendance at Grant's 10x boot Camp.

I had a unique opportunity to be surrounded by like-minded business professionals for three days as we shot questions to Grant. One question to Grant from a fellow attendee landed on "what books he reads to stay motivated or learn from on a daily basis." Several books were referenced however "Problems of Work" by Hubbard was one Grant said he leaned on the most. I know the book. I have taken the course. My favorite chapter is "Take a walk".

This was my chance to ask Grant about writing books. The day before he stated, "Don't write a book, finish a book". So, I asked, "Grant what is the best way to get started on finishing a book." That's where it all started.

To my surprise, Grant replied, "Today is Sunday at 1 pm. I'll give you until Friday at 2 pm to finish. If you do, we will sit down and talk about it together on a podcast." The entire room seemed stunned by his response which was followed by an outpouring of support by the other guests. An experience that will be with me forever. You have to be in the game to hit a home run, score a goal, or have a hole in one on the course so, off I went to start finishing my book.

The idea of writing a book about growing up in Charleston has long been with me, regaling my days as a tour guide, piloting a horse carriage, spinning tales of history and, of course, a few embellishments along the way to captivate the attention of my mainly-tourist audiences. As Grant states, "Never let the details ruin a great story."

And, then there were the college stories which made it nearly impossible to ever seek government office. And, my life as a chiropractor treating tens of thousands of patients in the South Carolina low country as well as a few Grammy winning, gold and platinum musicians and their bands. But, those stories would only serve the purpose of self-reflection and not serve the purpose of actually helping others or making a real difference in other people's lives.

In my own regenerative medical practice, our medical team strives to make real changes in people's lives by using the best products and services in the industry. My favorite service we offer is our Hormone Replacement Therapy in which we utilize testosterone, HCG, and estrogen blockers for men to reach their optimal levels.

Grant inspired me to take the knowledge and experience I have as not only a chiropractic physician but also as a patient to write a book on Hormone Replacement Therapy.

That book, TESTOSTERONE: BE BETTER IN THE BOARDROOM , BEDROOM, and the BALLFIELD was number 1 on Amazon Prime-Kindle and continues to educate those searching for answers since 2021.

Fast forward to the summer of 2021. I was approached by my childhood friend, Mr Brian Bilbro who challenged me to start researching information on how to naturally stop inflammation by using three components. Inflammation was at the forefront of what I pride myself in helping patients on a daily basis. In my quest for better health without the effects of chronic inflammation, I was excited to be able to learn about new research, ancient cures, and better ways to help others. A real opportunity to go out and really change the health of the world.

So, my purpose in writing a book on inflammaging is to help people gain an understanding on how inflammation causes serious lifelong disease conditions robbing us of a life full of happiness, and most importantly, HEALTH.

# Introduction

I have a rule in my practice. No patients are treated with any medical services unless I first receive them myself. Saying that, there is only one exception to that rule and that would be our female hormone programs. I am proud to say my amazing business partner and wife, Jessica Luckie was first in our office to be treated with that specific program.

For those old enough to remember the commercial that featured the president of Hair Club for Men on the TV saying, "I'm not just the president of the Hair Club for Men, I am also a client." Well, that's me. And that commercial has driven me to experience every service we bring into our medical office, first. One of my mentors back once shared in his deep, southern accent , "You gotta eat your own dog food." So, everyday in my practice you may see me receiving spa services, standing on a vibe plate, getting an adjustment, enjoying an IV treatment, and engaging with the team to encourage the same mindset.

My favorite program in our regenerative wellness practice is our men's hormone replacement therapy. Also known as TRT or Testosterone Replacement Therapy. In 2013, I was navigating an extremely stressful period with a Medicare audit, a failing marriage, and all of the stress that is accompanied therein. I was not sleeping well, I had no focus at the office, I was gaining belly fat, and losing muscle. I was in a brain fog. My zest for life felt like it had been stolen from me.

It was around that time I began researching the benefits of reducing chronic inflammation in the body and it occurred to me this was a potential avenue not only to improve my life but also to further my personal purpose of helping others. I had no idea just how much it would improve my life. I read and attended every course I could find and learned as much as I could about what supplements could reduce free radicals and thereby reduce oxidative stress and their ability to help people achieve optimal health. We all worked as a team to develop a system that was safe, affordable, and easy for any persian suffering from low energy, weight gain, brain fog, decreased libido, and not feeling like themselves. This book is dedicated to all those people who get up each and every day and make it happen for their families. The ones who push through when they are exhausted, under stress, and not living their best life. I'm here to tell you there is a better way. Your age doesn't have to be just a number. You can live well, well into your years. Stop allowing inflammation to rob you of a life. Start living and stop INFLAMMAGING right in its tracks.

# TABLE OF CONTENTS

"AGING is for those who don't know the SECRETS!"


Dr. Mark Luckie

# Chapter 1

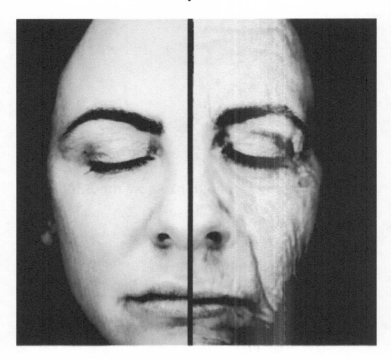

# INFLAMMAGING

Inflammation is Aging YOU

The mystery of inflammation begins from the start of man. And while I use the term "man" loosely, I can't help but think that a man was the first to experience inflammatory processes. Spraining ankles running from wild animals to the first man playing with fire to learning how to properly use rocks as tools-men, by nature, are not the smartest of creatures and injure themselves by doing some pretty stupid things. Even today the phrase, "Here, hold my beer usually ends up with some man in the ER with something broken, bruised, or bleeding.

Thankfully, most of us men have the support and love of the women in our lives including our moms, sisters, aunts, girlfriends, and wives. Saying that, we know that in fact both men and women were built with intrinsic, innate self healing properties to help protect us from injury, pathogen, and inflammation.

Inflammation is one of those properties. Inflammation is a critical and necessary part of the healing process. Not only does inflammation enclose an injured area for protection against viruses, bacteria, and debris but it can also call in your own stem cells and other regenerative cells to help repair the area. While inflammation helps the body, it can also be debilitating when in excess.

Due to the challenging times we faced from 2019 to 2021, inflammation has been dubbed as the word of the century since it is considered the primary cause of most, if not all, diseases. I liken it to that "recent unpleasantness."

Inflammation combined with early onset of aging is called INFLAMMAGING. A process where chronic, low grade inflammation causes cytokine storms and a whole host of dis-ease problems. Healthcare issues pertaining to inflammation continue to rise at an alarming rate which will certainly be taxing on the economy, the healthcare profession, the funeral homes, and our own family caregivers. And now inflammation is starting as early as childhood, severely affecting people as they age..

Most acute inflammation from injury or pathogens will clear from the body within a few weeks to a few months. It is when inflammation becomes prolonged (chronic) that it becomes detrimental to your health. Numerous healthcare providers have claimed that chronic inflammation is the underlying cause of all diseases.

Chronic inflammation has been defined as sterile, low grade inflammation in the absence of pathogens or injury that over-stimulates the immune system contributing to a wide variety of pathologies. Inflammaging is how inflammation becomes unregulated as one ages. While most researchers think of this as an older person's fate or as an aging process, it is my humble opinion inflammaging starts as soon as inflammation becomes uncontrolled. And, this can happen at any age. Evidence is emerging that the risk of developing chronic inflammation can be traced back to early development in life, and its effects are now known to persist throughout the life span to affect adulthood health and risk of mortality. (1,2,3)

Injury, whether acute or repetitive, exposure to irritants like; mold, pollen, dust, infection from pathogens, and auto-immune disorders all worsened by inflammatory lifestyles are ageless in nature. However, as one starts to age the innate capabilities to heal itself does become weakened due to loss of DNA repair mechanisms, pro-inflammatory cytokine secretion, mitochondrial damage, and an explosion of free radicals. All of these combined with several other factors like poor diet, sleep deprivation, sensory overload on social media, stress, inactivity, altered gut biome including disruption in mucosal barrier in the GI tract, and oxidative stress are all worsened as we reach midlife into our sunset years.

Knowing that (unregulated) chronic inflammation is worsened by lifestyle choices, environmental exposures, and a defect in the cells ability to heal itself, we must learn how to combat those detrimental factors in order to enjoy optimal health throughout our entire lives. In my practice, I have come to understand that most people believe a 3rd party is responsible for their health. Individuals feel powerless to make decisions regarding their own healthcare, often requiring the approval of their insurance company or medical practitioner. As a result, they may opt out of treatments that are more effective than pharmaceuticals simply because the treatment is not covered or deemed "unapproved" by a third-party payer or independent medical adjuster.

I truly believe in having a medical practitioner that not only listens but also is constantly studying, researching, and learning. One that educates but also is being educated. One that is not swayed by big pharma but has the patient's health at the forefront. All too often the "it's my way or the highway" approach is used in many of our healthcare facilities. This approach takes the patient out of their own choices and healthcare decisions.

It is important for individuals to take responsibility for their own health and become knowledgeable about the factors that contribute to chronic inflammation. Incorporating lifestyle changes like enhancing one's diet with the correct supplementation, boosting physical activity, managing stress, and limiting exposure to environmental toxins can significantly diminish chronic inflammation, consequently mitigating the effects of inflammaging..

Additionally, seeking out healthcare providers who prioritize patient education and work collaboratively with their patients can lead to more effective treatment and management of chronic inflammation. In the end, adopting a proactive stance towards managing inflammation by seeking guidance and care from various sources can culminate in enhanced health and well-being throughout an individual's entire life.

There is a common belief in our country that our bodies cannot heal without the help of medical doctors or insurance companies, which is far from the truth. While the medical community, especially emergency room medicine, is filled with dedicated professionals, the statistics indicate that our country is dealing with a significant healthcare crisis.

According to the WHO (World HEALTH ORGANIZATION):

The USA makes up 5% of the world's population.

75% of the world's pharmaceuticals are taken by the USA.

360 Billion dollars are spent on pharmaceuticals.

2 Trillion dollars are spent on healthcare coverage.

80% of pain medications like opioids are used by the USA.

The US infant death rate ranks 3rd worst among developed nations.

American life expectancy is 28th among 36 countries. (4)

If medications were the ultimate solution to our health issues, our country would arguably be the healthiest in the world. However, the reality is that we need to shift our approach to healthcare and address the root causes of illnesses. Since inflammation is believed to be the underlying cause of most diseases, it is crucial to focus on reducing chronic inflammation to improve our overall health.

Indeed, chronic inflammatory diseases have been recognized as the MOST significant cause of death in the world today, with more than 50% of all deaths being attributed to inflammation related diseases such as ischemic heart disease, stroke, cancer, diabetes mellitus, chronic kidney disease, non-alcoholic fatty liver, and autoimmune and neurodegenerative conditions. (5)

Inflammaging is costing much more than money to an already broken healthcare system. Inflammaging is robbing years off of our lives and certainly life out of our years. And those years are both chronological (actual age) and biological (physiologic age). It's true that the healthcare system in the US is facing some serious challenges and that there is a need for a new direction in thinking about health and wellness. Chronic inflammation is indeed a major contributor to many diseases and conditions, and addressing inflammation is a key factor in promoting overall health and longevity.

It's important to recognize that there are many factors that contribute to chronic inflammation, including lifestyle choices, environmental factors, and genetic predisposition. Addressing these factors requires a multifaceted approach that includes changes in diet and exercise habits, stress management techniques, and the best supplements that can help to reduce inflammation and promote healing.

At the same time, it's important to recognize the role that medical professionals can play in promoting health and wellness. While pharmaceuticals are not always the answer to health problems, there are cases where medications might be a part of a comprehensive treatment plan. Saying that, there is also a time and place for supplements to be incorporated into a patient's plan. It's important for patients to work closely with the right healthcare provider to develop a personalized plan that takes into account their individual needs and goals.

Ultimately, addressing the detrimental effects of inflammaging and the promotion of overall health and wellness requires a comprehensive, holistic approach that takes into account all aspects of a person's life. Collaboration among patients, healthcare providers, and caregivers can lead to the development of a healthier, livelier and more vibrant society for all people.

# Chapter 2
# CHRONOLOGICAL AGE vs BIOLOGICAL AGE

Age may be perceived as merely a number, but it holds significance in our health and wellbeing. In my practice, I have frequently encountered patients who experienced a decline in their physical and mental health once they hit the age of 50. Some have even visited me right after their 50th birthday, complaining of pain, discomfort, low energy, and a general feeling of unwellness. Many individuals have been informed that their bodies would react differently to life after turning 50, as if it were a magical age of decline. For other individuals, it appeared as though they were informed that turning 50 was the age when everything would start to fall apart, and unfortunately, some believed this to be true. As a result, this mindset may have contributed to their declining health.

It is essential to remember that words can manifest into thoughts, and thoughts can shape our reality. For some individuals, merely verbalizing that their body is starting to break down can be enough to convince themselves that it is happening. This thought process can lead to discomfort, fatigue, and eventually, the breakdown of the body. Inflammaging can begin to take effect, not just in the physical body but also in the mind. Inflammaging literally starts to happen right before their eyes, or should I say their minds?

But, again, does inflammaging have to age you as early as you are being told? I think not.

Your actual age is how long you have lived in chronological years. Biological age is the age of each of the 50 trillion cells and corresponding tissues based on physiologic evidence. (6) Rarely do these numbers ever match up due to the amount of stressors like toxins in our air, food, water along with repetitive or traumatic injuries. While everyone ages at different times, your healthspan can be extended where you are given the freedom from age-related diseases.

Maintaining good health and living a healthy lifestyle can positively impact one's cellular or biological age, potentially reducing it below their chronological age. On the contrary, living with chronic inflammation and poor health can accelerate one's biological age, resulting in a higher cellular age than their actual chronological age. Typically, individuals with poor lifestyle habits tend to have a higher biological age than their actual age.

The latest research shows that cellular health (biological) is much more accurate than your actual age (chronological) for predicting the onset of disease, ill-health, and ultimately, death. (7) The number of years you have spent on Earth cannot be adjusted. Since that is the case, how do you age gracefully in actual years while slowing down the process at a cellular level. What exactly can be adjusted to help your biological, cellular age? Have you ever met anyone who looked much younger than their age? Conversely, have you ever met someone who looked much older than their age?

## What were the differences?

### Skin Elasticity

### Energy Levels

### Mood

### Body Posture

### Physical Well-being

### Health of Hair

### Excitement for Life

While genetics play a role in how one ages, recent research suggests that external factors, such as lifestyle choices, can also have a significant impact on an individual's health and aging. Studies have shown that healthy lifestyle habits, such as exercise, maintaining a balanced diet, managing stress, and avoiding harmful substances like tobacco and excessive alcohol consumption, can potentially slow down the aging process at the cellular level. Additionally, factors such as exposure to environmental toxins and chronic inflammation can accelerate the aging process. It's important to note that while genetics can influence certain aspects of aging, external factors and lifestyle choices can still have a significant impact on overall health and aging.

These factors are what I like to call the 7 pillars of health.

Diet including clean air, food, and water

Exercise

Properly functioning spinal and nervous system

Sunshine

Positive Mental Attitude

## Stress Reduction

## Restful Sleep

These factors can influence the rate at which our cells age and can either accelerate or decelerate the aging process. For example, a diet rich in whole, unprocessed foods and antioxidants can help to reduce oxidative stress and inflammation in the body, which can contribute to lowering cellular aging. Regular exercise can also help to reduce inflammation and support the health of our cells and tissues.

On the other hand, chronic stress, poor sleep, and exposure to environmental toxins can accelerate cellular aging and increase the risk of age-related diseases.

By focusing on these pillars of health and making positive changes to our lifestyle habits, we can slow down the rate of cellular aging and potentially extend our health span. Thereby, reversing the effects of inflammaging.

So, while our chronological age is just a number, our biological age is a reflection of our lifestyle habits and the health of our cells and tissues.

# Chapter 3

Sugar is the gateway to AGEs

# Advanced Glycation End Products

One for the AGEs

"ONE for the AGES" is a term meaning memorable, long lasting, and noteworthy. For me, "ONE for the AGES" describes things like being backstage at a Prince concert, my first daughter Hannah's waterbirth, speaking in front of 7000 people, and last but not least, surprising my incredible wife Jessica with a wedding. Yes, it was a surprise for her and yes the surprise wedding was "ONE for the AGES".

And while this chapter on AGEs means something quite different, my hope is that the information here will become memorable and noteworthy in your quest for optimal health.

AGEs are Advanced Glycation End Products aka glycotoxins, yes they are as bad as they sound to your health. Advanced glycation end products (AGEs) are compounds that are formed when sugars react with proteins and lipids in the body. (8) This reaction, known as glycation, occurs naturally in the body and is a normal part of aging. (9) However, excessive formation of AGEs can contribute to various health problems, including diabetes, heart disease, and neurodegenerative disorders. Think of these newly formed compounds as sticky and gummy that can adhere to blood vessels clogging them causing the health issues mentioned previously.

AGEs are formed when sugars, such as glucose or fructose, react with amino acids in proteins or lipids. This process creates a complex chemical structure that can alter the function of proteins and lipids in the body, leading to tissue damage and inflammaging. This process happens in the absence of enzymes while causing irreversible and rearrangement reactions to increase one's cellular (biological) age.

AGEs can be produced within the body, as a result of normal metabolic processes, or can be derived from exogenous sources such as food. Foods that are high in AGEs include processed and grilled meats, fried foods, and high-fat dairy products. Cooking fatty proteins covered in sugary sauces on high heat increase the effects of AGES contributing to inflammaging.

Reducing the intake of foods that are high in AGEs and increasing the consumption of foods that are rich in nutrients, such as fruits and vegetables while also supplementing with the right antioxidants can help to reduce the formation of AGEs and mitigate their harmful effects. Cooking lean proteins slow and low with healthy oils, real butter, and limiting sugary condiments reduces the amount of AGES therefore bringing down one's biological age.

The NIH states dietary (d) AGEs increase oxidative stress, increase inflammation which leads to cardiovascular disease and diabetes.(10) This, in turn, leads to a whole host of negative feedback systems all causing inflammaging. By taking the right course of action you can drive down the number of AGES in your body.

# Chapter 4

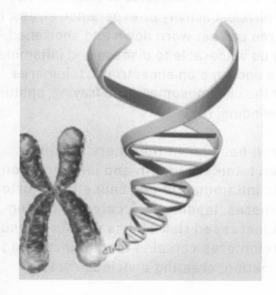

# TELOMERES

Telo-who? Telo-what? Telo-huh? Telomeres!

Telomeres are defined as the natural end of a chromosome composed of a long repetitive DNA sequence. You see, telomeres are like the bodyguards of our chromosomes. They protect our genetic information from damage, just like how you'd protect your home with a sturdy gate.

But here's the kicker – as we age chronologically, eat poor diets, are subjected to pollution, have lack of physical activity or experience stress, our telomeres can get worn down and shortened, leaving us vulnerable to disease and inflammaging. Like the end caps on shoestrings, telomeres protect the chromosomes from fraying, splitting, and unwinding. (11)

Research has shown that there is a link between telomere length and inflammation. Chronic inflammation can cause the shortening of telomeres, leading to accelerated aging and an increased risk of disease. As a result, short telomeres can also lead to increased inflammation, creating a vicious cycle.

One study found that individuals with shorter telomeres had higher levels of inflammation markers in their blood causing a myriad of issues including an increase in cancer. Cells with very short telomeres induced increased tumor necrosis factor1-α (TNF1-α) expression and senescence in larval tissues in a non cell autonomous manner, creating an inflammatory environment. (12) Another study found that age related decline in immunity is characterized by stem cell exhaustion, telomere shortening, and disruption of cell to cell communication leading to increased risk of disease. (13)

As we age or experience stress, our telomeres can shorten, making our cells more vulnerable to damage and disease. This process can affect our overall health and lifespan. That's why it's essential to take care of our telomeres and maintain their length.

But don't worry, there's good news! By taking care of our telomeres, we can actually slow down the aging process and improve our overall health. It's like having a secret weapon in our fight against aging! With the help of properly functioning and healthy telomeres, you'll discover how to optimize your health and live your best life possible.

By understanding the function of telomeres and how to keep them healthy, you'll discover how to optimize your health and unlock your best life possible. They play a crucial role in both our chronological and biological years.

That's right! Telomeres are incredibly important for maintaining our health and slowing down the aging process. By taking steps to keep our telomeres healthy and prevent them from shortening, we can improve our overall health and potentially extend not only our chronological age but our biological age as well. Some ways to take care of our telomeres include getting regular exercise, eating a healthy diet, managing stress levels, and avoiding harmful environmental factors like pollution and smoking. New research is showing there is a 2000 year old ancient vine that might also hold the key to lengthening the telomeres. And it might just be the cat's meow. Or, should I say the cats claw.

Take care of your telomeres and invest in your health. I encourage you to keep reading, more on this ancient remedy on Cats claw to follow.

# SOME FACTORS IN AGING

**Telomere Shortening**
chromosomes lose telomeres over time

**Chrono-logical Age**
risk factors increase over time

**Oxidative Stress**
oxidants damage DNA, proteins and lipids

**Glycation**
glucose sugar binds to and inhibits DNA, proteins and lipids

# Chapter 5
# SENESCENCE

Let's Make Sense of Senescence

Senescence refers to the process of biological aging, which is characterized by a progressive decline in the structure, function, and overall health of cells, tissues, and organs in the body. (14)

As we age, our cells undergo changes that can lead to senescence, which is a state of irreversible growth interruption caused by damage to the DNA, telomere shortening, oxidative stress, and /or inflammation.

Senescent cells can accumulate in the body over time and contribute to the development of age-related diseases, such as cancer, cardiovascular disease, and neurodegenerative disorders. These cells also produce proinflammatory molecules that can further damage surrounding tissues and contribute to the aging process as in inflammaging.

When cells become senescent, they stop dividing and enter a state of growth standstill. Think of these cells as "zombie cells" as they are old worn out cells that creep along in the body long after they die. These cells serves no purpse or function. These senescent cells also secrete a variety of molecules that affect nearby cells and tissues, and contribute to the development of age-related diseases. Senescent cells undergo extreme changes in gene patterns. They leak various bioactive molecules, which are associated with inflammation, and are referred to as the senescence-associated secretory phenotype (SASP).

Inflammation is a hallmark of senescence, and SASP can contribute to chronic inflammation in aging and age-related diseases. SASP factors can attract immune cells to the site of senescent cells, where their mission is to rid the body of macrophage.. However, if the immune response is not working properly , the accumulation of senescent cells can lead to a chronic low-grade inflammatory state, or "inflammaging," which can contribute to the development of many age-related diseases.

Furthermore, chronic inflammation can promote senescence by inducing DNA damage and telomere dysfunction, which can trigger the senescence response. This creates a positive feedback loop, in which inflammation induces senescence, and senescence, in turn, promotes inflammation, perpetuating the cycle. The age old question of "which came first"? Either way both inflammation and senescent cells cause inflammaging of the body.

In organisms, senescence can manifest in a variety of ways, such as a decline in physical and cognitive function, increased susceptibility to disease, and a reduced ability to repair and regenerate tissues. Other symptoms of an overload of senoscence cells would be increased joint stiffness, longer recovey times after excercise, and declining physical energy.

While senescence is a natural process that occurs in all organisms, there are ways to potentially slow down or delay the onset of age-related changes. Maintaining a healthy lifestyle, such as exercising regularly, eating a healthy diet, and avoiding harmful environmental factors like smoking, can all help support healthy aging. Aging is for those who don't know these secrets.

Researchers are also exploring various interventions to target senescence and potentially slow down the aging process, such as astaxanthin that can selectively eliminate senescent cells from the body.

In summary, senescence and inflammation are intimately linked, and both play important roles in aging and age-related diseases. Strategies to reduce senescent cell burden and inflammation may promote healthy chronological and biological aging while encouraging disease prevention.

# Chapter 6

## Free Radicals aren't Free

Few things in life are actually free. And while that may be true, I believe the absolute best things in life are free: sunrises, hugs, smiles, sunshine, sunsets, and friends to name a few. And while those things are all free and radical, the term free radical is not free or radical. Free radicals come at a high cost and for some free radicals can lead into an unhealthy path of disease processes.

Free radicals are unstable, unpaired electrons produced by the exchange of oxygen. Free radicals are molecules that are unbalanced, making them highly reactive and able to damage cellular components such as DNA, proteins, and lipids. Free radicals are produced as byproducts of normal cellular processes, such as the exchange of oxygen and energy production, and can also be generated by exposure to environmental toxins such as pollution and cigarette smoke.

I liken free radicals to that unstable drunk girl at a party. You know the one. That person who is bouncing around trying to find someone, anyone to hang on too. Unstable, unpaired, and trying to hold on for dear life. Free radicals act the exact same way as the drunk person at the party These unstable electrons want to become stable by pairing up. They try to become stable by stealing electrons from stable atoms, damaging the cell in the process. Making matters much worse is this process of stealing electrons they create more unstable atoms, setting into place a very harmful reaction. This leads to large scale cellular damage fanning the flame to increase more free radicals increasing the chance for dis-ease in the body.

HEALTHY ATOMS          FREE RADICALS          ANTIOXIDANTS

While these free radicals wreak havoc on the body, there is great news. Your body has an innate, self healing immune system that is designed to protect us from free radicals, and, in turn, from disease processes. The function of this system and its mechanisms is dependent on a delicate balance between oxidants and antioxidants. When it's balanced, the body is more than likely to be in homeostasis. When there is an imbalance of free radicals and antioxidants, the body is in a state of oxidative stress. Oxidative stress has been shown to activate the main gene marker for inflammation called NF-kB, setting off a cytokine storm. (15)

Oxidative stress is an imbalance of antioxidants to free radicals (oxidants) in the body. Free radicals are produced from normal, human bodily functions that most of us take for granted everyday like breathing, exercising, eating, and just living and enjoying life. In short, as we live life our cells are producing energy in the mitochondria, the powerhouse of the cell.. Think of mitochondria as the power plant and like all power plants they produce energy in the form of ATP. The by-product of energy production in the cells is free radicals. In fact, this process of exchanging oxygen for energy is considered to be the main source of free radical development. (16)

Once generated, free radicals impact not only the structure of the cells but also the function of the cell. This comes at a high price: free radicals are not free. Once the mitochondria's function is in decline it severely affects the energy production and significantly increases mitochondrial free radical production. (intechopen.com) An increase in free radical production in the absence of the correct anti-oxidants causes inflammatory responses while altering immune function, opening the way for the development of many disease processes. In fact, free radicals are costly to the body in the form of oxidative stress and ultimately, to the entire healthcare system's financial wellbeing. And yes, healthcare is a big business. Actually, it should be called free radical care as many disease processes have been linked back to oxidative stress which is taxing our healthcare system.

Oxidative stress is known to be involved in the development and progression of numerous diseases. While it is difficult to provide an exact number, it is estimated that oxidative stress is linked to more than 200 diseases and conditions, including:

Cancer

Cardiovascular diseases (such as atherosclerosis, hypertension, and heart failure)

Neurodegenerative diseases (such as Alzheimer's, Parkinson's, and Huntington's disease)

Diabetes

Autoimmune diseases (such as rheumatoid arthritis and lupus)

Chronic obstructive pulmonary disease (COPD)

Asthma

Kidney disease

Liver disease

Eye diseases (such as age-related macular degeneration)

Antioxidants can help neutralize free radicals and prevent oxidative damage. Additionally, consuming a diet rich in fruits and vegetables, which contain antioxidants and other beneficial compounds, can also help reduce oxidative stress.

"However, since our endogenous antioxidant defenses are not always completely effective, and since exposure to damaging environmental factors is increasing, it seems reasonable to propose that exogenous antioxidants could be very effective in diminishing the cumulative effects of oxidative damage. Antioxidants of widely varying chemical structures have been investigated as potential therapeutic agents. However, the therapeutic use of most of these compounds is limited since they do not cross the blood brain barrier (BBB)." (17)

Therefore, an antioxidant taken exogenously that crosses the BBB is needed by every person on the planet. The great news is new research shows one to do just that while also protecting and supporting the mitochondria, and it's called Astaxanthin.

Lifestyle factors such as exercise, stress management, and avoiding environmental toxins can also play a role in reducing free radicals and, in turn, reducing oxidative stress while promoting optimal health. Regular physical activity has been shown to increase antioxidant defenses and reduce inflammation, while stress reduction techniques such as meditation and mindfulness may also have beneficial effects on cellular health.

In summary, maintaining a balance between oxidants and antioxidants is important for overall health and wellness in order to decrease free radical damage. Consuming a diet rich in fruits and vegetables, exercising regularly, and practicing stress management techniques are all important ways to reduce oxidative stress and promote optimal health. Also, consuming an antioxidant that crosses the Blood Brain Barrier to help stave off numerous disease processes is vital to your health.

# Chapter 7

TODAY'S QUOTE:

*Friends don't let friends have Oxidative Stress*

- a concerned friend

## OXIDATIVE STRESS

**Oxidative stress is a condition that occurs when there is an imbalance between the production of**

reactive oxygen species (ROS) and the ability of cells to detoxify or repair the damage caused by these ROS. ROS are natural byproducts of cellular metabolism, and they play important roles in cellular signaling and defense against pathogens like viruses and bacteria. However, when ROS levels become excessive, they can cause damage to cellular structures, including the cellular wall and mitochondria, leading to cellular dysfunction and ultimately, cellular death. (18)

There are several factors that can contribute to oxidative stress, including exposure to environmental toxins, radiation, and certain medications. Lifestyle factors such as poor diet, lack of exercise, and stress can also increase ROS production and contribute to oxidative stress.

Oxidative stress has been linked to the development of several diseases, including cardiovascular disease, cancer, and neurodegenerative disorders. Additionally, oxidative stress has been implicated in the biological (physiological) aging process. Oxidative stress ages you. Another factor in inflammaging.

To counteract oxidative stress, the body has several mechanisms to neutralize ROS and repair cellular damage. These include enzymes such as superoxide dismutase, catalase, and glutathione peroxidase. (19) Antioxidants also provide protection against oxidative stress.

The relationship between oxidative stress and inflammation is complex, and it is not always clear which came first in a particular disease process.

In some cases, oxidative stress can trigger an inflammatory response. For example, when reactive oxygen species (ROS) are produced in excess, they can damage cellular structures and activate pro-inflammatory signaling pathways. This, in turn, can lead to the release of cytokines and other inflammatory molecules, initiating an immune response.

On the other hand, inflammation can also contribute to oxidative stress. When immune cells are activated in response to an infection or injury, they produce ROS as part of the normal immune response. However, excessive inflammation can lead to the production of more ROS than can be detoxified or repaired by the body, leading to oxidative stress.

Overall, it is likely that oxidative stress and inflammation are mutually reinforcing processes, with each contributing to and exacerbating the other in a feedback loop. Understanding the relationship between oxidative stress and inflammation is important for developing strategies to prevent and treat diseases associated with these processes, such as cardiovascular disease, cancer, and neurodegenerative disorders.

# Chapter 8

## Cytokine Storm and Path of Destruction

Growing up in Charleston, I have always had a fascination with storms including hurricanes. These super storms powered by warm waters are always highly destructive and never predictable. Their path is anyone's guess even though we have the best meteorologist with their high tech equipment flying right dab smack in the eye of the storm. Depending on the size of the storm, the tightness of rotation of the eye, wind speed, air temperature at landfall, pressure decibels and a few more variables that are out of my sphere of knowledge hurricanes leave cities big and small unrecognizable.

A cytokine storm in the body is not much different. These storms are also destructive and unpredictable driven by an overstimulated immune system wreaking havoc in the body. Even though we have the best in medical technology, how the cytokine storm affects each individual is still a mystery. For some, the symptoms may be non-existent and for others it could be life ending. Either way, the path that the cytokine storm causes damage thru inflammation.

Cytokine storm is a severe immune reaction in which the body releases an excessive amount of cytokines, which are signaling molecules that help regulate the immune response. The cytokine storm can occur in response to a variety of triggers, including infections,autoimmune diseases, Covid-19 with spike proteins, and other inflammatory disease processes. In a cytokine storm, the immune system can become overactive and attack healthy tissues and organs, leading to serious and potentially life threatening complications. The body actually goes into attack mode not recognizing itself and attacks healthy cells. Symptoms of a cytokine storm can include fever, inflammation, respiratory distress, organ failure, and shock. (20 )

The treatment for a cytokine storm often involves controlling the underlying cause trigger, such as treating the infection or controlling the inflammation and their pathways. The key is to control the immune response and prevent further damage to the body.

Cytokine storm and inflammation are related but distinct concepts. Inflammation is a normal and necessary part of the immune response to infections, injuries, and other types of tissue damage. It involves the release of cytokines and other signaling molecules that attract immune cells to the site of damage and help to initiate the healing process.

However, in some cases, the immune system can become overactive and lead to excessive inflammation, which leads to tissue damage and other complications. This is where the cytokine storm can wreak havoc on the body. So while inflammation can be a natural response to a pathogen or tissue damage in an acute injury, cytokine storm is an excessive and potentially dangerous overreaction of the immune system. Cytokine storms can occur in response to a variety of triggers, including infections and autoimmune disease.

NF-kappa B is a protein complex that plays a key role in regulating the expression of genes involved in the immune response, inflammation, and cell survival. It is activated in response to a variety of stimuli, including cytokines, pathogens, and cellular stress. (21)

Cytokine storm and NF-kappa B are also related but also distinct concepts. Think of them as kissing cousins. Cytokine storm is a severe immune reaction in which the body releases an excessive amount of pro-inflammatory molecules, leading to widespread inflammation and tissue damage. NF-kappa B is one of the key signaling pathways that regulates the production of those cytokines, including the ones involved in cytokine storms. When NF-kappa B is activated, it sets off the production of cytokines and other immune system molecules that help to fan the flames of the immune response which promotes more inflammation. However, if NF-kappa B becomes overactive or unbalanced, it can lead to excessive cytokine production and contribute to the development of cytokine storms.Therefore, NF-kappa B is an important player in the development as well as the disruption of a cytokine storm, and controlling its activation and regulation is a potential therapeutic target for alleviating its harmful effects.

Inflammation is a complex process that involves the activation of various immune cells and the release of signaling molecules such as cytokines, chemokines, and growth factors. NF-kappa B is a critical regulator of the inflammatory response as it triggers the production of pro-inflammatory cytokines that recruit immune cells to the site of inflammation. NF-kappa B is present in an inactive form in the cytoplasm of cells, bound to inhibitor proteins. Upon activation, the inhibitor proteins are degraded, allowing NF-kappa B to translocate to the nucleus and bind to DNA, thereby promoting the expression of genes involved in the inflammatory response. (22)

However, the disruption of NF-kappa B activity can lead to excessive and chronic inflammation, which is implicated in the pathogenesis of many diseases such as cancer, autoimmune disorders, and chronic inflammatory conditions. While targeting and switching off the NF-kappa B gene marker may provide a powerful therapeutic strategy for eliminating inflammation and related diseases, one must also consider a combination of approaches, including lifestyle modifications, including diet, supplements and exercise routines, as well as biologic therapies that target specific cytokines or immune cells.

By calming the path of the cytokine storm and switching off the gene marker for inflammation one would be able to stave off inflammatory processes while helping the cell's biological age. In other words, by calming the storm through an anti-inflammatory (preferably one without side effects), the body would age better, people would live healthier and longer lives. Score another one for fighting the ill effects of inflammaging.

# Chapter 9
# B. Y. O. G

Bring your own guts

## "ALL DISEASE BEGINS IN THE GUT"
### -Hippocrates

Scientific studies, researchers, healers, and scholars including Hippocrates all point to the gut as being where disease starts and where the healing process can begin. Ulcers, colitis, leaky gut syndrome, IBS, and other gut related diseases like life-threatening allergies can not only be debilitating but can be presented as incurable diseases from the medical establishment. "Just learn to live with it!" Is a sentiment heard all too often today in many healthcare facilities around the country.

However, the current era of the information age enables individuals to access a plethora of resources such as research studies, TikTok videos, and personal accounts from people worldwide who aspire to improve their physical and mental well-being. This collective desire to improve one's quality of life involves adopting a healthier lifestyle, and it reflects a significant change in people's mindset. Instead of merely masking their symptoms with medication, individuals are seeking to identify and address the root cause of their health concerns.

Looking to the gut as a starting point for the healing process is becoming increasingly important in today's healthcare market, as it involves addressing the root cause of health issues instead of just treating symptoms with drugs. "With 70-80% of immune cells being present in the gut, there is an intricate interplay between the intestinal microbiota, the intestinal epithelial layer, and the local mucosal immune system. In addition to the local mucosal immune responses in the gut, it is increasingly recognized that the gut microbiome also affects systemic immunity." (23)

When the gut microbiome is not functioning properly it directly affects the breakdown of foods and, in turn, affects the immune system. If the lining of the gut is allowing undigested, small food particles into and through it many issues like "leaky gut syndrome", crohn's disease, IBS, and other gastrointestinal issues may arise.

"Studies suggest a relationship between factors (eg, foods and bacteria residing in the intestine), the epithelial lining, and the mucosal immune system. Rearrangement of tight junction proteins in the small bowel and colon leading to increased intestinal permeability have been observed. These abnormalities are thought to contribute to the outflow of antigens through the leaky epithelium, causing overstimulation of the mucosal immune system. Immune factors, released by these cells, including proteases, histamine, and prostanoids, participate in the perpetuation of the permeability dysfunction and contribute to the activation of abnormal neural responses involved in abdominal pain perception and changes in bowel habits.

Probiotics are an attractive therapeutic option in IBS given their recognized safety and by virtue of positive biological effects they can exert on the person . Of importance for the IBS pathophysiology is that preclinical studies have shown that selective probiotic strains exhibit potentially useful properties including anti-inflammatory effects, improvement of mucosal barrier homeostasis, beneficial effects on intestinal microbiota, and a reduction of visceral hypersensitivity." (24)

The connection between the gut and mental health is becoming increasingly recognized by healthcare professionals. The gut contains millions of nerve cells that communicate with the brain through the nervous system, and research has shown that the gut can impact mood, behavior, and even cognitive function. In fact, many neurotransmitters, such as serotonin and dopamine, are produced in the gut, which can affect mood and emotions. Thus, improving gut health can also have a positive impact on mental health. (25)

Research has also shown a link between gut health and chronic diseases such as diabetes, heart disease, and even cancer. Poor gut health can lead to chronic inflammation, which is a common factor in many chronic diseases.

Fortunately, there are steps that can be taken to improve gut health and promote overall wellness. One of the most important steps is to focus on a healthy diet, rich in whole foods and fiber. This can help to promote the growth of beneficial gut bacteria, which can support the immune system and improve overall health.

Other strategies for improving gut health include managing stress, getting enough sleep, and avoiding exposure to environmental toxins. Prebiotics, probiotics, and digestive enzymes can also be helpful in supporting a healthy gut microbiome. We must not forget the lining of the gut as well. Collagen peptides can be a factor in the healing as well.

In summary, the gut is a critical part of the body's overall health and wellness. By focusing on gut health and taking steps to improve it, we can support the immune system, reduce inflammation, and potentially reduce the risk of chronic diseases. All of which can decrease one's cellular age to continue to fight inflammaging.

# Chapter 10
# Blood Panels

### And You get a Blood Test

Similar to how Oprah exclaims, "You get a car! And you get a car! And you get a car!" I strongly advocate for regular blood tests, saying, "You get a blood test! And YOU get a blood test! And, you get a BLOOD test!" Why? Because it's important to assess if you are experiencing chronic, low-grade, sterile inflammation without realizing the potential consequences.

It is common knowledge to recognize a sprained ankle by the pain, limited range of motion, heat radiating from the affected area, and the inflammation causing swelling. Similarly, the severity of back pain can also be an indicator of inflammation and easy to detect, just as easy as a sprained ankle. In my personal practice, I have observed that patients tend to become more conscious of inflammation as the severity of their injury increases. The larger the source of pain, the more noticeable and palpable the inflammation tends to be.

But what about the subtle, low-level inflammation that is not accompanied by visible symptoms or pain? How can one detect its presence?

The question can be summarized as: how can you detect if your body is deteriorating due to low-level inflammation that is not easily detectable?

Is it possible to detect inflammation at an early stage, treat it, reverse its effects, and prevent it from recurring? Are there cost-effective tests that can be conducted periodically to monitor one's inflammatory status on a scale?

Numerous individuals have undetected low-level inflammation in their bodies, which they are unaware of because they do not experience any symptoms. However, seemingly minor issues such as gingivitis can escalate into major problems throughout the body.

The misconception that you appear healthy on the outside despite harboring internal inflammation is a major self-deception. Unfortunately, low-level inflammation is not easily detectable and often goes unnoticed while going about daily routines such as brushing teeth, fixing hair, or selecting clothing.

Although chronic low-level inflammation is common, it is not a normal state. Therefore, determining your baseline level of inflammation could be one of the most crucial tests you can conduct. Thankfully, these tests are readily available, affordable, and most physicians are familiar with them and should be able to order a panel for you.

Nonetheless, these tests have their limitations. They can reveal the presence of inflammation in the body, but not its location or cause. Nonetheless, being aware of the existence of inflammation is the initial step in addressing it. Moreover, if the tests indicate an absence of inflammation, it would be useful to know which tests can confirm this. From there, we can move on to finding solutions to correct and prevent inflammation.

Let's take a look at a few of the simple blood tests you can request in your local doctors offices.

## ESR

The term ESR stands for erythrocyte sedimentation rate. It is a non-specific test for detecting inflammation in the body, indicating its presence but not its origin. The ESR test is a well-established and reliable method of testing for inflammation.

To perform the test, your red blood cells are placed in a tube, and as they clump together, they gradually settle to the bottom of the tube. This process is known as sedimentation. The speed at which the red blood cells settle indicates the level of inflammation present in the body.

Here are the ranges for ESR.

The normal range for ESR (erythrocyte sedimentation rate) can vary depending on a person's age, sex, and other factors. In general, the normal range for ESR is as follows:

For men under 50 years old, the normal range is 0-15 mm/hr

For women under 50 years old, the normal range is 0-20 mm/hr

For men over 50 years old, the normal range is 0-20 mm/hr

For women over 50 years old, the normal range is 0-30 mm/hr (26)

The higher the number the more the inflammation. It's as simple as that. The test is affordable, easy, and accurate.

So you can easily check to see if things like your lifestyle; diet, exercise programs, stress management, or supplements are helping to reduce your inflammation by starting with a baseline.

## CRP

CRP stands for C-reactive protein. Like ESR, a CRP test will tell you that inflammation is present but not where the location of the inflammation is originating.

This test is significant because it measures the inflammation marker from the liver. The liver secretes enzymes and proteins when inflammatory markers are turned on. One of these proteins is CRP and, in fact, it's one of the earliest proteins present with inflammation. Saying that, it can detect inflammation early on, C-reactive protein (CRP) levels can increase due to various conditions such as infections, autoimmune disorders, cardiovascular disease, and other illnesses. Many healthcare professionals utilize CRP testing to assess the risk of atherosclerosis, as there is a link between internal inflammation of the vascular walls and the adherence of cholesterol to the interstitial tissue walls. (27)

- The normal range for CRP (C-reactive protein) can vary depending on a person's age, sex, and other factors. In general, the normal range for CRP is as follows:

- For a healthy adult, the normal range is less than 10 mg/L. (28)

A test known as high-sensitivity CRP (hs-CRP) has been developed and is believed to be capable of detecting inflammation at an earlier stage. Nevertheless, research has shown that CRP is just as reliable and significantly more cost-effective for individuals. The usual laboratory tests for CRP values in the lower range highly correlate with the hs-CRP tests and can therefore replace the costlier hs-CRP measurements.(29)

Note:As a healthcare provider and a caring husband, I consider this test to be extremely significant for myself and my family. My incredible wife had been suffering for over a year and a half, and was eventually diagnosed with undetected Lyme disease and exposure to mold. I believe that her symptoms were brought to the forefront by a seemingly mild to moderate case of SARS-CoV-2, which she had contracted earlier. These symptoms included sleeplessness, brain fog, forgetfulness, and an overall sense of malaise. While some might argue that these are common symptoms experienced by many mothers on a daily basis, the constant and intense itching in her ears, headaches, and complete exhaustion made me realize that something had to be done.

Jessica received treatment from several practitioners who were all experts in their respective fields. After completing her treatment, our nurse practitioner, Kelly Delaney, had the insight to order a CRP panel during a hormone and thyroid blood test. Jessica"s test results revealed significant levels of inflammation, indicating that it was likely the root cause of their health issues. See below for the initial test.

Working closely with me and our nurse practitioner, we were able to develop a plan to address the inflammation and improve their overall health. Part 2, titled "The Fix," outlines the steps taken to support her journey towards better health. Indeed within a few months you can clearly see the amazing results Jessica obtained here:

# INFLAMMAGING

**Luckie, Jessica**
Patient ID:
Specimen ID: 356-022-0077-0

DOB:
Age: 37
Sex: Female

**Patient Report**
Account Number:
Ordering Physician: **K DELANEY**

● labcorp

## Luteinizing Hormone(LH) (Cont.)

Postmenopausal 7.7 - 58.5

## FSH

| Test | Current Result and Flag | Previous Result and Date | Units | Reference Interval |
|------|------------------------|--------------------------|-------|--------------------|
| FSH[01] | | | mIU/mL | |

Adult Female:
Follicular phase 3.5 - 12.5  Ovulation phase 4.7 - 21.5  Luteal phase 1.7 - 7.7  Postmenopausal 25.8 - 134.8

## Prolactin

| Test | Current Result and Flag | Previous Result and Date | Units | Reference Interval |
|------|------------------------|--------------------------|-------|--------------------|
| ▼ Prolactin[01] | | | ng/mL | 4.8-23.3 |

## Estradiol

| Test | Current Result and Flag | Previous Result and Date | Units | Reference Interval |
|------|------------------------|--------------------------|-------|--------------------|
| Estradiol[01] | | | pg/mL | |

Adult Female:
Follicular phase 12.5 - 166.0  Ovulation phase 85.8 - 498.0  Luteal phase 43.8 - 211.0  Postmenopausal <6.0 - 54.7  Pregnancy 1st trimester 215.0 - >4300.0 Roche ECLIA methodology

## Vitamin D, 25-Hydroxy

| Test | Current Result and Flag | Previous Result and Date | Units | Reference Interval |
|------|------------------------|--------------------------|-------|--------------------|
| Vitamin D, 25-Hydroxy[01] | | | ng/mL | 30.0-100.0 |

Vitamin D deficiency has been defined by the Institute of Medicine and an Endocrine Society practice guideline as a level of serum 25-OH vitamin D less than 20 ng/mL (1,2). The Endocrine Society went on to further define vitamin D insufficiency as a level between 21 and 29 ng/mL (2).
1. IOM (Institute of Medicine). 2010. Dietary reference intakes for calcium and D. Washington DC: The National Academies Press.
2. Holick MF, Binkley NC, Bischoff-Ferrari HA, et al. Evaluation, treatment, and prevention of vitamin D deficiency: an Endocrine Society clinical practice guideline. JCEM. 2011 Jul; 96(7):1911-30.

## C-Reactive Protein, Cardiac

| Test | Current Result and Flag | Previous Result and Date | Units | Reference Interval |
|------|------------------------|--------------------------|-------|--------------------|
| ▲ C-Reactive Protein, Cardiac[01] | 19.82  **High** | | mg/L | 0.00-3.00 |

Relative Risk for Future Cardiovascular Event  Low <1.00  Average 1.00 - 3.00  High >3.00

57

# Dr. Mark Luckie

**Luckie, Jessica**
Patient ID:
Specimen ID: 089-022-0411-0

DOB:
Age: 38
Sex: Female

**Patient Report**
Account Number:
Ordering Physician: K DELANEY

labcorp

Date Collected: 03/29/2023 | Date Received: 03/30/2023 | Date Reported: 03/31/2023 | Fasting: **Not Given**

Ordered Items: **C-Reactive Protein, Cardiac; C-Reactive Protein, Quant**

Date Collected: **03/29/2023**

## C-Reactive Protein, Cardiac

| Test | Current Result and Flag | Previous Result and Date | Units | Reference Interval |
|---|---|---|---|---|
| C-Reactive Protein, Cardiac [01] | 2.09 Relative Risk for Future Cardiovascular Event  Low <1.00 1.00 - 3.00  High >3.00 | | mg/L Average | 0.00-3.00 |

## C-Reactive Protein, Quant

| Test | Current Result and Flag | Previous Result and Date | Units | Reference Interval |
|---|---|---|---|---|
| C-Reactive Protein, Quant 012mg/L0-10 | | | | |

**Disclaimer**
The Previous Result is listed for the most recent test performed by Labcorp in the past 5 years where there is sufficient patient demographic data to match the result to the patient. Results from certain tests are excluded from the Previous Result display.

**Icon Legend**
Out of Reference Range Critical or Alert

**Performing Labs**
01: BN - Labcorp Burlington 1447 York Court, Burlington, NC, 27215-3361 Dir: Sanjai Nagendra, MD
For Inquiries, the physician may contact Branch: 843-996-1175 Lab: 800-762-4344

Patient Details Physician Details Specimen Details
**Luckie, Jessica**K DELANEYSpecimen ID: **089-022-0411-0**
**2 CARRIAGE LN, CHARLESTON, SC,West Ashley Wellness And**Control ID: **L2302035517**

58

## **FERRITIN**

Ferritin serves as a gauge of iron levels within the body. Although iron deficiency is prevalent among women and individuals with low iron intake, it may escape detection in mild instances. Inadequate iron levels in the bloodstream constitute iron deficiency, which can adversely impact the capacity of red blood cells to convey oxygen to bodily tissues. Thus, iron serves as a crucial component for optimal cellular function.

Symptoms of low iron include:

Extreme fatigue, weakness, malaise, cold extremities, brittle nails, pale skin, and of course, inflammation.

Although ferritin is commonly linked to low iron levels, it can also serve as an indicator of chronic inflammation. Prolonged inflammation can lead to increased levels of ferritin in the body. However, it is important to note that high ferritin levels do not always suggest inflammation.
It could be due to an excess of ferritin.
Therefore, relying solely on this test to diagnose inflammation may not be accurate, and additional tests may be necessary.

The normal range for ferritin in your blood serum is: 24 to 336 ng/mL for adult males. 24 to 307 ng/mL for adult females. (30)

Conclusion:

- Low ferritin levels indicates low iron levels not inflammation.

- Normal ferritin levels equates to good iron levels but does not signify having or not having inflammation

- High ferritin levels signifies too much iron or chronic inflammation.

Although these three tests are readily available and cost-effective, they are not the sole markers that can be examined. In the event that the results of these three tests indicate abnormally high levels, additional testing for antibody, IL-6, and TNF alpha can be requested. These tests are designed to specifically evaluate immune function and assess how the body is responding to inflammation.

# Chapter 11
# Supplements Matter

"Let food be thy medicine, and medicine be thy food."

Hippocrates

With a plethora of information about health and wellness products on the market today, from social media platforms to television commercials to the local gym enthusiast, it is no wonder why there is so much misinformation about supplementation for optimal health.

For some, the word supplements create visions of large, hard to swallow capsules to very unpleasant tasting shakes leaving one wondering if any of it makes a real difference in their healthcare journey. Adding to the equation is the conundrum that some health and wellness products are actually made (created) in a lab using coal tar or petroleum. These synthetic supplements are cheaper to create, make more money for unscrupulous companies, and some even create health issues.

Our bodies were not designed to recognize vitamins and minerals in the form of supplements created by scientists in lab coats. Furthering the misinformation are the laws created to protect these companies' advertising rites knowingly they do not support the truth in advertising.

The abundance of misinformation in the health and wellness industry has left many individuals feeling confused and uncertain about how to make informed decisions about their health. In addition, the rise of social media influencers promoting products that are often driven solely by monetary gain has only added to this confusion. This is especially concerning because people may turn to these products as a quick fix after consuming alcohol, edibles, and high-carbohydrate foods while binge-watching their favorite shows late at night, potentially leading to negative consequences.

Kristina Kajic, President of a Direct Sales-Influencer Model company called Bella Grace says, "Too many people have unrealistic expectations when it comes to marketing products online. Many times the goods and services are over promised and they underperform. While influencing models continue to rapidly expand into the billions, it is important to understand the quality of products you are consuming. Not every product is equal for everybody." Kajic goes on to say, "In a fast paced world where anyone can put a name on a product, it is extremely important to make sure you are aligning yourself with your health goals while choosing the right supplements." Social selling and influencing marketing is on track to grow to 1.2 trillion dollars in the next 2 years. Ms. Kajic is proud to say her company is using science based components backed by years of professional research and development for the future.

When the unscrupulous marketing tactics of certain companies are coupled with a medical profession that pays little attention to the body's natural ability to heal itself through proper nutrition, including vitamins, minerals, and supplements, clean water, a well-functioning nervous system, and exposure to sunlight, it's not astonishing that the United States is one of the world's most unhealthy nations, with its high obesity rate leading to heart disease, diabetes, and numerous other related illnesses.

The word of the century, inflammation, lies at the core of all these disease processes. When inflammation is coupled with early aging, it is referred to as Inflammaging, a condition in which chronic low-grade inflammation triggers cytokine storms and a range of health issues. Problems in healthcare, such as the surging prevalence of obesity, are increasing at an alarming pace, which will undoubtedly put a strain on the economy, healthcare professionals, funeral homes, and our own family caregivers. Furthermore, our children are now being severely impacted.

Poor diets, poor water quality, poor air quality along with a barrage of chemicals, pesticides, and microplastics have stressed our gut and immune health to their limits. Recent studies have discovered that microplastics have infiltrated not just our lung tissue but also the very walls of our cells. As per research findings, 75% of those tested have been shown to have microplastics in their bodies. These tiny particles have been linked to a variety of detrimental effects on human cells, including allergic responses and cellular death. (31)

All of these toxins are stressing our immune systems to their limit. Stress comes in many forms on the body. Some stress causes headaches, anxiety, allergies, and low back pain which all tax the nervous system. For others stress shows in our bodies in the form of generalized pain, inflammation, and pre-aging caused by an imbalance of free radicals and antioxidants.

# INFLAMMAGING

For many health-conscious individuals, the primary objective is to discover a suitable combination of high-quality supplements that combat inflammation, alleviate nervous system stress, and aid in restoring the body's balance. Once this combination is achieved, it can be the key to a happier, healthier life filled with purpose, joy, and vitality – a life that frees you from the negative impact of chronological and biological aging, and eliminates the adverse effects of inflammaging.

# INFLAMMAGING PART 2
# THE FIX

There is now no doubt that free radicals initiate oxidative stress, which is further exacerbated by inflammation via the NF-kappa B pathway. This can lead to a cytokine storm in some individuals, damaging telomere length and ultimately reducing cellular health and accelerating biological aging. Consequently, our cellular age may be far exceeded by our chronological age. This is the recipe for INFLAMMAGING! Wow! Read that again.

At the root of the problem is inflammation.

What do we do about chronic inflammation? Is there a way to stop inflammaging in its tracks?

What exactly are the necessary supplements and strategies to help you stop inflammaging, and age naturally without the effects of many of the lifestyle disease processes.

Collagen, astaxanthin, and cat's claw exhibit extraordinary antioxidant and anti-inflammatory properties, which collectively contribute to reducing the likelihood of inflammaging. Each of these three substances contains essential components that are effective in mitigating inflammation and oxidative stress.

Collagen peptides are a protein variety that originates directly from collagen, the primary structural protein in the body. Astaxanthin, on the other hand, is a carotenoid pigment that can be found in specific types of algae. Its potent antioxidant properties allow it to safeguard cells against damage induced by free radicals. Finally, cat's claw is an herb native to the Amazon rainforest that comprises various compounds that exhibit anti-inflammatory characteristics.

Incorporating cat's claw, astaxanthin, and collagen into your daily routine can aid in reducing oxidative stress by eliminating free radicals which consequently lowers the likelihood of INFLAMMAGING.

# Chapter 12

Collagen. It is everywhere. They put it into everything. I would not be surprised if it started to show up in baby formula, cereal, or in our potato chips. You can find collagen in Costco, Wal-Mart, large department stores, and even in drug store lotions. Individuals have been persuaded to incorporate collagen into their coffee, apply it to their skin, nasal spray or even opt for injections. However, the question remains – does any of it truly make a difference? Are these companies genuinely concerned about our overall health, or is it simply a ploy to profit by promoting low-quality collagen through attractive marketing schemes?

Let's do a deep dive to find out more about collagen.

Collagen has been called the glue that holds everything together. The root word for collagen is Kolla which is Greek for glue. Collagen is the main structural protein found in the body's various connective tissues. Collagen supports the matrix of the skin, hair, nails, teeth, bones, connective tissues, GI tract, interstitial tissue, as well as organ tissue. Gram for gram, collagen is stronger than steel. It makes up approximately 40% of the protein in your body, 70% of the protein in your skin, and 80% of the protein in your bone. In fact, collagen is the most abundant protein found in the body. Twenty-eight types of collagen have been identified with Type I , Type II, and Type III making up 90% of collagen types. While Type 1 supports hair, skin, nails, bone and tendons/ligaments, Type II supports cartilage health, and Type III supports arteries and intestines.

Collagen makes up 80% of our skin and works along with elastin to make our dermis layer smooth, supple,and elastic. (32)

Collagen production naturally begins to decline in our 20s, and lifestyle choices and environmental factors can accelerate that decline. While collagen is an essential protein that provides structure, elasticity, and strength to our skin, bones, muscles, and other tissues, it is important to learn how to not only maintain your collagen matrix but how to stimulate more production from your own body.

Smoking, excessive sun exposure, poor sleep, an unhealthy diet, and pollution are all factors that can contribute to premature aging and a reduction in collagen production. Smoking, in particular, can cause oxidative stress and inflammation, which can damage collagen fibers and lead to sagging, wrinkles, and other signs of INFLAMMAGING.

UV radiation from the sun can also damage collagen fibers and reduce collagen production, INFLAMMAGING and an increased risk of skin cancer. Knowing the right time of day and the right natural sunscreens are important for protection. Poor sleep quality and a diet lacking in essential nutrients can also contribute to a reduction in collagen production and accelerate the aging process. Environmental factors such as pollution can also contribute to oxidative stress and inflammation, which can damage collagen fibers and lead to more of the same, INFLAMMAGING.

It is important to take care of your skin and overall health to maintain collagen production and prevent premature aging. This can include wearing natural sunscreen, avoiding smoking, getting enough sleep, eating a healthy diet, and minimizing exposure to environmental toxins. Additionally, some skincare products, treatments, and supplements may help to stimulate collagen production and improve the appearance of aging skin, brittle hair and nails,

Many people reach for the latest fad of swallowing collagen in any form that is available. A great deal of these collagen products only provide the bare minimum of bioactive proteins in their formula. Meaning that they do not use those peptides that truly make a difference in one's well being. Far too often companies use the "Type" as a marketing tool and ploy to convince the public to buy and consume their product.

A lot of individuals have been convinced that by ingesting a certain "type" of collagen, it will miraculously substitute that identical collagen type in their system. Dr. Mark S Miller states, "Believing that swallowing something else to replace something that was lost is simply untrue. That thinking is actually absurd. The body does not interpret types of collagen that way."

Collagen is naturally tough and gristly, with protein chains that are too large to be properly digested in the small intestine. This is why pure, complete collagen is rarely used. Instead, collagen peptides are utilized because they can be digested efficiently and reassembled correctly. According to Dr. Miller, this process is similar to a pearl necklace, where the chain represents the complete collagen and the individual pearls represent the smaller peptide chains of 2 or 3 amino acids. These smaller peptide chains are already in a form that can be digested by the small intestine. Dr. Miller explains that these shortened chains can pass through the intestines easily, similar to a wine key penetrating a cork.

However, just delivering these amino acids through the small intestines is not enough to make collagen (in its various forms) because making the protein is tightly regulated.

Collagen production, as with any protein, is regulated by the presence and activity of specific enzymes that are responsible for coding the protein. These enzymes, or processes, are activated only when necessary and become dormant when they are not needed. It's important to note that each type of collagen has its own unique enzyme, or gene, that is responsible for constructing it. (33)

After the absorption of amino acid and peptide chains in the small intestine, the subsequent steps are crucial in achieving the two primary mechanisms of action that assist the individual. The first mechanism is to prevent the breakdown of collagen in the body. The second mechanism is to stimulate the body's fibroblasts to produce additional collagen. (34)

Now let's take a look at how these collagen substrates have been used in marketing over the past few years to get collagen into the health and wellness space. Dr. Miller uses the term generational collagen products and how they are all like IKEA furniture.

Dr. Miller likens this to building IKEA furniture. In what he labels as the 3 generations of collagen that have been marketed to the general public.

Generation 1

Collagen is delivered but with no instruction and no enzymes to help it along in collagen production. Imagine building an IKEA desk with zero instructions and no tools.

This is the current state of affairs for the majority of the collagen industry, with results that are inconsistent and leave some consumers unsatisfied. To compensate for this flaw, marketing efforts often focus on differentiation, such as emphasizing the origin of the collagen (e.g., marine, bovine, chicken, etc.) or the type of collagen used.

Here is a range of sources of Collagen on the market, but are they equivalent? Let's break down their characteristics.

## *Marine*

- Derived from fish scales/skin and jellyfish

- It is the cheapest form available, so companies like to promote it

- Devoid of clinical support to validate its effectiveness

- Often pre-digested (hydrolysed) to make it soluble

## *Bovine*

- Generated from cow hide and hoofs

- Available in various forms of complexity & support

- Pre-digested for solubility and absorption

- Clinical support limited to certain branded bioactive peptides

### Chicken

- Obtained from rooster combs and egg membranes

- Minimal clinical research documenting benefits

### Vegan

- Not actually Collagen, but small peptides created from fermentation processes to mimic structures in Collagen.

- Devoid of clinical research to determine its utility and effectiveness

- An amino acid cocktail using the collagen name for marketing purposes (35)

However, focusing solely on the differentiation of "types of collagen" is a diversionary tactic and does not address the fundamental problem. They are akin to playing with the cardboard box in which the furniture was delivered and building a "fort" out of it. As a result, it's important to note that these first-generation collagen products lack clinical trial support for the desired outcomes.

## Generation 2

In the second generation of collagen products, the collagen is absorbed and effectively stimulates fibroblasts to produce additional collagen. This is a significant step towards building the desired "Ikea furniture," but while these branded collagen peptides are effective in providing the necessary instructions to the fibroblasts, their impact is limited. This indicates that the process is functional but not operating at its maximum capacity. More skilled help is needed to complete the full task.

In addition, it's worth noting that second-generation products may contain other components or ingredients that provide benefits beyond just skin health. While this is undoubtedly valuable and can serve as a point of differentiation, there is still much more that can be done to promote health and achieve beauty from within to ultimately fight inflammaging.

## Generation 3

3rd Generation of Collagen Health products are where outcomes are advanced through an intimate knowledge of the science that is involved.

It is built on a solid appreciation of how tissues respond to stress, utilize nutrients and how to rebalance systems that may be out of alignment.

The antioxidant and gene-switch activities of astaxanthin and cat's claw alter the balance in favor of collagen construction, resulting in improved skin health. Cat's claw is a very effective inhibitor of the recruitment of MMPs, and like astaxanthin, actively stimulates the enzymes that make collagen.

As a result of their actions, these additional elements enable superior decision-making and a more reliable utilization of ingested collagen peptides, leading to more predictable outcomes. (36)

According to Dr. Miller's studies, the most effective collagen source for achieving optimal outcomes is Verisol B collagen from Gelita. This collagen has been extensively researched, with 10 human clinical trials conducted on both its safety and efficacy. As a result, Verisol B collagen is considered the best collagen product available on the market.

The VERISOL®B (bovine) brand is a highly selected range of peptides that do more than supply critical amino acids to make collagen, VERISOL®B (bovine) activates skin cells (Fibroblasts) to generate locally Collagen and other matrix elements.

VERISOL®B (bovine) Is made from Collagen derived from bovine as it selects the most important peptides to optimize skin health Global leader in providing clinical support validating its benefits on Collagen and matrix metabolism to promote skin health, appearance, function and form. (37)

When asked about the best collagen, Dr. Miller responds with a smile and says, "Why, of course, human collagen is the best." However, he clarifies that he is not referring to ingesting human collagen. Rather, he means using specific peptides, coded enzymes, and other factors to stimulate an individual's own natural production of collagen. Dr. Miller considers this approach to be brilliant because it promotes the body's natural ability to produce collagen, which can decrease inflammation and restore beauty from within, leading to optimal health outcomes.

What benefits does collagen play in our overall health?

## HAIR, SKIN and NAIL HEALTH

Collagen can help your skin become firmer, increase smoothness, decrease fine line wrinkles by improving skin elasticity while decreasing cellulite. Collagen can enhance follicle thickness and help prevent baldness.

- VERISOL® leads to significantly higher skin elasticity – up to 15 % – compared to placebo treatment. This effect could be measured after just 4 weeks of treatment and persisted after 8 weeks of oral VERISOL® administration. Another 4 weeks after the last intake of the product, VERISOL® application still showed higher skin elasticity levels than in the placebo treated group. (38)

- The study shows a decrease of cracked and/or chipped nails after 2 months of treatment, reaching a decrease of 42 % after 6 months. Compared to the control group, the nail growth speed is increasing. VERISOL® led to a statistically significant improvement in nail growth after 3 months of treatment. At the same time, there's a notable improvement in nail peeling and a clearly decreased nail edge irregularity. 80 % of the patients were completely satisfied with VERISOL® treatment. 75 % of the women perceive their nails as longer, 71 % said their nails grow faster and become longer. (39)

## REDUCES JOINT DISCOMFORT

Degradation of collagen causes joints to be less supple, stiff, achy, and loose motion. Collagen provides the matrix needed for support and repair. (40)

## REPAIRS LEAKY GUT

Collagen lines the entire Gastro-intestinal tract.

"The types of collagen produced by human intestinal smooth muscle cells in culture were the same as those collagens extracted from structured human bowels (types I, III, and V). These findings suggest that collagen production by human intestinal smooth muscle cells has a role in the repair as well as the fibrosis of the gastrointestinal tract." (41)

## HEART HEALTH

Collagen peptides are believed to support heart health by supporting the strength of the blood vessels by providing structure to the arteries. Research supports the benefit of heart health by showing a significant increase in the plasticity of the interstitial tissues (arteries) while also boosting the amount of good cholesterol. (42)

## MUSCULO-SKELETAL HEALTH

Collagen makes up 40% of the protein found in the body which includes 10% found in our muscle mass. A large portion of collagen is also found in our bones whereby the collagen matrix promotes mineralization. Unfortunately as we age our bodies lose the ability to produce collagen by way of our fibroblasts. Reports show that 1% of collagen is lost yearly after the age of 25. By the age of 75 we have lost over 50% of our collagen causing joint discomfort, weakness in tendons and ligaments,and low bone density which leads to brittle bones, fractures and osteoporosis.

Without a good supply of collagen stimulating peptide chains your musculoskeletal system cannot perform properly. Studies show men who supplemented with collagen while engaging in a workout program showed significant improvements in muscle mass and joint function. (43)

## WEIGHT MANAGEMENT

When collagen production is lowered and tendons, ligaments, and joints are not supple people tend to not want to make any additional movements like walking, riding bicycles, jogging, or exercising,

While collagen may not be the next weight loss sensation, it does provide nourishment to the musculoskeletal system while supporting a healthy metabolism. This increase in energy to the body leads to stronger, more effective workouts which lead to more activity. More activity when combined with a healthy diet and proper water intake leads to weight management.

Collagen, however, does help with cellulite reduction as shown in a research with Verisol B collagen.

- A double blind, randomized, placebo-controlled study with 105 women aged between 25 and 50 years shows that the daily oral intake of 2.5 g VERISOL® significantly decreases the cellulite score. The effect was measured after 3 and 6 months supplementation. VERISOL® has a beneficial effect on skin extracellular matrix and restores the normal structure of the dermis and subcutaneous tissue. VERISOL® supplementation also reduced the waviness of the skin, with first results visible after 3 months, but more pronounced after 6 months. With a daily dose of 2.5 g VERISOL® the appearance of cellulite women with a BMI < 25 was significantly reduced. (44)

# Chapter 13
# Astaxanthin

Hard to pronounce, easy to swallow

If Budweiser is the King of Beers, Elvis is the King of Rock n Roll, and Richard Petty is the King of Nascar Racing, then Astaxanthin is King of Antioxidants. Astaxanthin is a superpowered antioxidant with anti-inflammatory properties that has special anti-aging benefits to the body. Antioxidants are classified by their mode of actions depending on their enzymatic and non-enzymatic activities, water and/or fat solubility, and their ability to donate electrons (primary) or oxygen scavenging (secondarily). Astaxanthin, however, is not only in a class by itself, it plays on a totally different ballfield. Astaxanthin has extremely unique and different properties, and because Astaxanthin is so unique and different this antioxidant often gets more results than any other antioxidant. Astaxanthin antioxidant properties are proven to be 6000 times stronger than Vitamin C, 3000 times stronger than resveratrol, 800 times stronger than CoQ10, 500 times stronger than Vitamin E, 350 times stronger than green tea extract, and 100 times stronger than Vitamin D. (45)

Dr Mark Miller, Astareal Astaxanthin company's global ambassador , has not only researched astaxanthin but has presented his findings all over the world including his latest research on "Astaxanthin – The Ultimate Mitochondrial Nutrient for Performance & Recovery".

Dr. Mark Miller states, "There are many actions of astaxanthin that are difficult to replicate with other natural products, either in breadth, potency or specificity. Firstly, it is a pre-eminent free radical scavenger, and here this action is pure. In other words, while it functions to quench the unpaired electron that constitutes a free radical, astaxanthin in of itself does not become a free radical. This potent action means that astaxanthin is very effective at limiting oxidative stress across many sources e.g., UV radiation (eyes, skin), mitochondrial dysfunction or inflammation."

Dr. Miller's research shows astaxanthin modifies gene expression throughout the body. "This epigenetic action restores balance to a wide range of genes involved in tissue repair (activates) and inflammation (suppresses). Astaxanthin has positive actions on metabolism, limiting lactic acid accumulation and promoting endurance."

"Finally, Dr. Miller adds, astaxanthin has truly desirable actions as a pre-eminent mitochondrial nutrient, where it limits the oxidative stress resulting from dysfunctional, leaking mitochondria, whilst taking off-line these damaged mitochondria (mitophagy) and replacing them with new healthy ones. Critical actions that make astaxanthin an essential nutrient for healthy aging." (46)

Let's look at the features, advantages and benefits of Astaxanthin and how it can support a healthy lifestyle.

Astaxanthin Features:

1) Both water soluble and lipid (fat) soluble carotenoid

2) Pure antioxidant

3) Has multiple free electrons to fight more free radicals at once

4) Can fight more than one free radical at once

5) Can cross the BBB (blood brain barrier) and the BRB (blood retinal barrier)

6) Acts upon multiple inflammatory pathways decreasing oxidative stress

## Astaxanthin Advantages

1) Protects the entire cell both inside and outside as it forms protective bridges and scavenges free radicals

2) Never turns into a pro-oxidant (free radical) in the body.

3) Neutralizes free radicals without becoming depleted

4) Can fight multiple free radicals at once thereby reducing oxidative stress

5) Neurotropic qualities offer superior protection to the brain, eyes.

6) Decreases inflammation

## Astaxanthin Benefits

1) Nurtures and nourishes all 50 trillion cells in the body.

2) No risk of toxicity in the body.

3) Last longer in the body for more antioxidant fighting power.

4) Most powerful antioxidant in the body.

5) Improved cognitive and eye function.

6) Anti-aging properties by reducing oxidative stress.

7) Reduces inflammation in the body

8) Improves male fertility

Astaxanthin's unique characteristics make it the most powerful, virtually unmatched yet least known antioxidant. Because it is water and lipid soluble, astaxanthin protects both the inside and the outside of the cells forming bridges and scavenging free radicals.

Let's take a look at a few individual ways Astaxanthin helps with some of the most common yet most destructive disease processes in the body.

## DIABETES

Diabetes is one of the most detrimental health issues our country faces today. Diabetes affects millions of Americans often causing loss of eyesight, loss of limb, and an end of life care that is miserable to those affected by it as well as those family members chosen to help manage it. But, there is new research showing promise in using astaxanthin.. Astaxanthin reduces blood glucose by metabolizing sugar in the blood. This function, in turn, increases sensitivity to insulin and helps regulate blood sugar levels. The weight management and reduction in LDL cholesterol numbers from astaxanthin also help in managing diabetes. (47)

## WEIGHT LOSS (MANAGEMENT)

Weight management involves two basic concepts when taking on losing unwanted pounds. One is consuming less calories and the second is burning more calories. New research is showing astaxanthin helps with the latter in two ways: 1) by metabolizing fat, and 2) by increasing muscle endurance and then by helping recovery after workouts.

By metabolizing fats, astaxanthin helps the body burn cleaner energy thereby decreasing free radical output. By helping with endurance and recovery, astaxanthin helps burn more fat while allowing the exerciser to enjoy a better, more rewarding experience. (48)

## HEART DISEASE

Heart disease is the number one killer in the United States according to the CDC. Heart disease kills about 600,000 people yearly and is responsible for 1 out of 4 deaths. The productivity and effectiveness of the heart muscle decreases when lifestyle choices cause free radical accumulation due to a lack of antioxidants. (49)

Astaxanthin may help the heart in several different ways. Astaxanthin may prevent plaque build-up which promotes better blood flow in arteries, improves lipid profiles, and reduces oxidative stress by decreasing inflammation. A study in 2006 showed Astaxanthin thickens the walls of the blood vessels thereby reducing blood pressure. (50)

## OSTEOARTHRITIS AKA DEGENERATIVE JOINT DISEASE

OA or DJD is a term loosely used for painful, stiff joints that most believe happens in old age. Many people go to bed with Arthur and wake up with Ben. That is they go to bed with arthritis and wake up with Ben Gay.

However, osteoarthritis is NOT an age related disease process. Read that again. Osteoarthritis is NOT an age related process. While some chronologically aged people suffer with OA, it isn't their age. It's the way the body repaired or actually didn't repair after an injury.

You may not believe me. I will prove it to you. The next time someone says "my shoulder hurts" or "my knee hurts" or "my elbow hurts" and "It must be my age" ask them how old the other (same) body part's age is? It's a simple concept. If one's age had something to do with pain and stiffness, EVERY knee, shoulder, elbow, wrist and joint of their body hurt . It would if, in fact, chronological (actual) age was the issue.

OA or DJD is actually a disease process of joints that were injured one time or injured repetitively over time causing the biological age (physiologic age) to be decreased. Either way the joint is not moving properly and now waste products are not moving out and nutrition is not moving into the area. This lack of motion starts the breakdown of the joint.

Astaxanthin may help by supporting and supplying new cartilage cells to damaged joints. By reducing the inflammation in the joint, astaxanthin may help painful, swollen joints by allowing the person to move better. Better movement and more motion helps joints heal.

## **MENTAL HEALTH**

Mental health encompasses a wide range of conditions that affect our mood, our thinking, and our behavior. Our mental health determines our emotional well-being, psychological well-being and our social well being. It drives what we think, what we do, and how we act in every setting throughout every stage of our lives. Mental health is synonymous with cognitive behavior. Our thought processes become our reality. "Every human being is the author of his own health or his own disease." says Buddha.

This quote puts the responsibility on the individual and not on a third party company.

Shinedown, arguably the greatest rock-n-roll band with 20 number 1 hits on the Billboard charts, has tackled the topic of mental health based on their own personal experiences and by listening to the stories of their millions of fans. Both the lead singer Brent Smith and Eric Bass have struggled in the past and use those experiences to write music. The song " GET UP" on the self produced award winning album ATTENTION ATTENTION is one of those songs. While the song was originally inspired by Bass, Smith says the "song represents something much more than just battling clinical depression; instead, it represents not being afraid of your failures in life." Smith is a firm believer in that people are never defined by their failures, and failing is never the end of the world. He believes it to be quite the opposite, in that you're going to be defined by never giving up. Whether they are playing in front of a small house or 500,000 people, the message is still the same. Smith says don't be afraid of failing as it teaches you what to do next time. "Your life and your legacy will be built by the foundation that you refuse to never give up." So, GET UP, GET UP, GET UP!

From my own personal experiences in practice and studies on the human body , it appears that a lack of mental clarity and focus can have serious consequences on a person's well-being. This issue may originate from the cellular level and can lead to negative outcomes. Cells that are clogged with inflammation damage mitochondria. Mitochondria produces energy. New research from the UConn School of Medicine reported in the American Journal of Geriatric Psychiatry that adults with major depression often have rapidly aging mitochondria. (51) We have seen it in immune cells, in glial cells in the brain, in adipose tissue. We see a systematic cellular change in depressed older adults, says one of the researchers, meaning overall, older adults with major depression show accelerated aging in cells throughout their body.

Essentially what they are saying is chronic, widespread inflammation damages mitochondria which affects every living cell, tissue, organ, and system in the body.

Astaxanthin was found to have a positive effect on depressive-like behavior in pre-clinical trials. Its ability to cross the lipid wall of the cell and set up by the mitochondria to support it at a high level. The benefits were associated with both its anti-inflammatory and antioxidant properties.

# Chapter 14
# CATS CLAW

Does not come from cats

This chapter is dedicated to my sweet, southern mother.

Bless her heart. While driving home from a conference in Florida, I received an urgent call from my mother. "Mark, I need to know –I am allergic to cats. I noticed I am taking cat claws. Will this cause me to have allergies? I think one of the claws scratched my throat." I seriously almost wrecked the car. I have been spreading the benefits of Cats claw for many, many months publicly. Surely, this wasn't real and she was joking. But alas, it wasn't a joke.

Needless to say, my Mother justifiably received more than one cat present for Christmas. And probably more with each holiday season to come.

Fear Not, there are NO cat claws in Cats Claw Cat's claw (uncaria tomentosa) aka Uña- de gato is a wild, native vine that grows in tropical regions mainly in Central and South America. This woody vine with claw-shaped thorns grows into the canopy of the rainforest expressing beautiful, trumpet-like yellow flowers. It is a popular herbal supplement that is believed to have various health benefits, such as reducing inflammation, boosting the immune system, and aiding in the treatment of certain conditions like arthritis and digestive problems.

The indigenous tribes of Latin America have used Cat's claw for over two thousand years warding off all kinds of health problems from asthma, arthritis, gastric ulcers, insect stings, and inflammattion. Many tribes used Cat's claw to help new mothers recover from childbirth, deep wound healing, and to clean out the kidneys. The bark, roots, and leaves were boiled down and used in their medicinal treatments. While some tribes used Cats claw to heal the body, others used it to help with mental and spiritual aspects of the body in traditional ceremonies.. The shamans had many names for this healing vine, one being the Helper Herb and another being The Life Giving Vine of Peru.

Coming into the modern era, Cat's claw has been used to support a wide range of ailments due to its anti-inflammatory and antioxidant boosting properties including arthritis, gastritis, menstrual cycles, osteoarthritis, viral infections, AIDS and other immune deficiencies , and there are some researchers studying the benefits of its cancer killing capabilities.

Arguably the world's best researcher on Cats claw, Dr. Mark S Miller states, " Cat's claw has been a passion of mine for over 20 years following my many excursions into the Amazon Rainforest in search of new therapeutics for diseases and disorders. A focal point of my academic research was to listen to how the locals manage their health (note little is written in the Amazon, experience is passed on orally) and with thousands of questions I could decipher not only potential mechanisms of action but also the general properties of the active ingredients (chemical). It was a journey of discovery and more than a few misadventures." (52)

I have had the unique opportunity to interview Dr. Miller on several occasions. Not only is he brilliant but his Amazonian rainforest stories are filled with fun, laughter, and intrigue.

Dr. Miller goes on to say Cat's claw was his first success on this journey of discovery. " Indeed, I was able to crack the code of exactly how it works within 6 weeks. More important than our expediency (it was not always like that) was the mechanisms of action, which was a Holy Grail target for chronic inflammation – suppression of the master gene switch, NF-kB. This switch controls thousands of genes that contribute to inflammation and it was a highly sought after developmental target in drug development. Not only did Cat's claw work via this marvelous action, it was magnificently potent and from my reading it remains the most potent inhibitor of this switch. It is able to prevent macrophage production of TNFalpha (regulated by NF-kB)." (53)

Dr. Miller went right to work and published multiple pubmed studies on the efficacy of the anti-oxidant and anti-inflammatory properties on Cats claw. One such study titled **Cat's claw inhibits TNFalpha production and scavenges free radicals: role in cytoprotection** found cat's claw is an effective antioxidant, but perhaps more importantly a remarkably potent inhibitor of TNFalpha production. The primary mechanism for cat's claw anti-inflammatory actions appears to be immunomodulation via suppression of TNF alpha synthesis. (54)

Another remarkable study by Dr. Miller on the anti-inflammatory results on Knee OA (osteoarthritis) stated, Pain associated with activity, medical and patient assessment scores were all significantly reduced, with benefits occurring within the first week of therapy. " The study also found Cats claw had NO deleterious effects on blood or liver function or other significant side-effects compared to placebo. (55)

These findings are significant as they found Cat's claw to have an inhibitory effect on NF-kappaB pathway, which is one of the mechanisms by which it may reduce inflammation. By inhibiting NF-kappaB activation, this leads to the arrest of pro-inflammatory cytokines, such as interleukin-1 (IL-1) and tumor necrosis factor-alpha (TNF-alpha), and in turn, decreases the chances of the development of chronic inflammatory diseases.

But Cat's claw may also provide more benefit than only as an inflammatory. There is some scientific evidence to suggest that Cat's claw may have the potential to support DNA repair. (56) DNA repair is a critical process that helps to maintain the integrity and stability of our genetic material, which can be damaged by oxidative stress in rats with induced arthritis, potentially by inhibiting the activation of NF-kappa B.

# Chapter 15
# SEVEN PILLARS of HEALTH for ANTI-AGING

I always discuss the 7 pillars of health with my patients when they inquire about achieving optimal health, anti-aging, and making the most out of their lives. It simply comes down to the SEVEN pillars of health : 1) clean air, water, and food including vitamins, supplements and minerals, 2) exercise, 3) properly functioning nervous system, 4) sunshine, 5) positive mental attitude, 6) stress reduction, and 7) restful sleep. These 7 pillars of health when used can have an immediate, positive result in one's immunity and self-healing capabilities. Thomas Edison, a founding forefather, was quoted as saying "The doctor of the future will give NO MEDICINE, but will interest his PATIENTS in the care of the HUMAN FRAME, diet and in the CAUSE and PREVENTION of disease." - Thomas Edison

If you read the quote closely, you can see Mr. Edison was clearly ahead of his time in his forward thinking about healthcare.

## CLEAN AIR, CLEAN WATER, and CLEAN FOOD

We have all heard the commercials, "Did you serve or live at Marine Corps Camp Lejeune between 1953 and 1987? You may have been exposed to contaminated tap water with harmful chemicals known to cause health problems. Call us today to see if you qualify for compensation."

In today's environment, our bodies are constantly being exposed to toxins in the water and our air. To this day nine years later Flint, Michigan residents are bathing and using water that smells of chemicals or dirty feet. Many Michiganders don't trust the water system and are being exposed to dangerous lead levels even to this day.

Our air supply isn't much different. Long term health effects from air pollution include heart disease, lung infections, and respiratory diseases due to the inflammation. This pollution can take the form of gasses, solids, or liquid droplets. Air pollution is most concentrated in heavily populated cities due to the smog caused by emissions from transportation, factories, and chemicals being used in and on everything.

Toxins found in our air, water, and our food affect our immune system in an extremely negative manner.

Air purifiers are a great way to clean the surrounding air space. Personally, I like a dual purpose ozone-blue light air purification system. But, it doesn't stop with that. Diffusing good quality essential oils is also soothing to the body, and the lungs.

Drinking water from cheap plastic bottles should never be an option. As I stated on the nationally syndicated Bobby Bones show, plastics leach phthalates into our bodies disrupting our hormones causing more inflammatory issues.. The solution is to use BPH free containers. Put Ph balanced water at 9.0 from a reverse osmosis or distilled water machine Food free from poisons, toxins, and/or additives is extremely important. Eat clean. Learn the skills needed to grow your own organic vegetables. Shop at local farmers markets. Ask questions about their farm. Stay out of the middle of the grocery stores for food. This is where you find foods full of artificial dyes, colorings, and additives to make you crave more.

## EXERCISE:

Exercise has many benefits that work together with the other pillars of health. Exercise can aid in weight management, improve sleep, promote better sexual experiences, improve mood, and also helps combat health conditions.

Michaal Dosher, PT of Dosher Physical Therapy located in the upstate of SC says, "Proper joint motion while exercising plays a huge role in keeping your body young and healthy." Dosher, a personal friend of mine since we were young boys playing sports at St. Andrews Playground, goes on to say, "Exercise helps move inflammation out and nutrition into the joint tissue. It is an important part of a healthy lifestyle. He agrees while acute inflammation starts the healing process, chronic widespread inflammation wreaks havoc on bodily systems." I wholeheartedly concur with an individual with whom I have spent several years playing on the ballfield, practicing with the Middleton Singers, and enjoying double dates with our respective girlfriends.

## PROPER FUNCTIONING NERVOUS SYSTEM:

The supreme system in the body is the central nervous system. The CNS comprises the brain and the spinal cord. Both the brain and the spinal cord are surrounded by bone for protection. The skull protects the brain. The spinal cord is surrounded and protected by 24 movable spinal bones. A properly functioning spinal system protects and helps the nervous system express 100% health. Keep your spinal system moving properly and your nervous system will thank you. Working with a chiropractor, an exercise physiologist, massage therapist, and a physical therapist will put years on your life and life on your years.

## SUNSHINE:

Sunshine is needed by every living person on the planet. I am baffled at the amount of parents who unknowingly lather their children in poisons daily by using mass and chemically produced sunscreens. The skin is our largest organ and can certainly absorb what is constantly layered upon it. Keep the sunscreens natural and get 20 minutes of morning or late afternoon sun.

Sunshine provides loads of benefits: reduces stress, improves sleep, maintains strong bones, maintains healthy weight, staves off depression, and also strengthens the immune system.

## POSITIVE MENTAL ATTITUDE:

Maintaining a positive mental attitude can have significant benefits for aging individuals. individuals, including improved physical health, cognitive function, and overall well-being.

A positive mental attitude can also have potential benefits for anti-aging. Aging is a natural process that occurs in all living organisms, and while it cannot be stopped, the rate of aging can be influenced by various factors, including psychological factors.

One of the key ways in which a positive mental attitude can contribute to anti-aging is by reducing stress. Chronic stress has been linked to accelerated aging and a range of age-related diseases, such as cardiovascular disease, cognitive decline, and cancer. When we have a positive outlook on life, we are better able to manage stress and cope with challenges, which in turn can slow down the aging process.

Additionally, a positive mental attitude can lead to healthier lifestyle choices, such as engaging in regular exercise, maintaining a healthy diet, and avoiding unhealthy habits like smoking or excessive drinking. These healthy lifestyle choices can help to prevent age-related diseases and maintain physical and cognitive function.

Research has also shown that a positive mental attitude can improve immune function, which can play a role in anti-aging. The immune system is responsible for fighting off infections and diseases, and as we age, it can become less effective. However, studies have found that individuals with a positive mental attitude have stronger immune systems and are less susceptible to infections and diseases.

In conclusion, a positive mental attitude can potentially contribute to anti-aging by reducing stress, promoting healthy lifestyle choices, and improving immune function. While aging is a natural process that cannot be stopped, maintaining a positive outlook on life can help to slow down the aging process and improve overall health and well-being.

## STRESS REDUCTION:

Stress reduction is an important aspect of healthy aging. Chronic stress can lead to the accumulation of free radicals, which can contribute to cellular damage and increase the risk of age related diseases. Additionally stress can negatively impact sleep quality which is essential for the body's natural processes of repair and rejuvenation. Chronic stress can also affect the levels of cortisol, a hormone produced by the adrenal glands that help the body manage stress. (57) Over time, high levels of cortisol can have negative effects on the body, including decreased bone density, impaired immune function, and increased risk of cardiovascular disease. Therefore, it is important to develop strategies for managing stress as a part of a healthy aging plan. This can include regular exercise, mindfulness practices such as meditation, or yoga, social support, and engaging in enjoyable activities.

## RESTFUL SLEEP:

Restful sleep is important for overall health and well-being, and it can also have significant anti-aging benefits. During sleep, the body repairs and rejuvenates itself, including the skin, which is the largest organ in the body. Here are some ways in which restful sleep can contribute to anti-aging:

1. Reduces inflammation: Inflammation is linked to numerous age-related diseases, such as diabetes, heart disease, and Alzheimer's disease. Sleep deprivation has been shown to increase inflammation in the body, while restful sleep can help to reduce it.

2. Improves skin health: During sleep, the body produces collagen, which is essential for maintaining healthy skin. Collagen helps to reduce wrinkles and fine lines, as well as improve skin elasticity.

3. Enhances cognitive function: Sleep plays a crucial role in memory consolidation and learning, which are important for maintaining cognitive function as we age. Restful sleep can help to improve cognitive function and prevent age-related cognitive decline.

4. Boosts immune function: Sleep is also essential for the proper functioning of the immune system. It helps to produce immune cells that fight off infections and diseases, which can contribute to anti-aging.

5. Regulates hormones: Hormones such as growth hormone and cortisol are important for overall health and well-being, and they are regulated during sleep. Restful sleep can help to maintain a healthy hormonal balance, which can contribute to anti-aging.

In conclusion, restful sleep is crucial for anti-aging as it helps to reduce inflammation, improve skin health, enhance cognitive function, boost immune function, and regulate hormones. It's important to prioritize good sleep habits, such as maintaining a consistent sleep schedule, creating a relaxing sleep environment, and avoiding stimulants like caffeine and electronics before bedtime.

Thomas Edison's quote emphasizes the importance of taking a holistic approach to healthcare and focusing on prevention rather than just treating symptoms with medicines. The Seven Pillars of Health- clean air, water, and food; exercise, properly functioning nervous system, sunshine positive mental, stress reduction, and restful sleep – are all important components of a healthy lifestyle that can help prevent disease and promote optimal health. By focusing on these pillars and making healthy choices in our daily lives, we can support our body's natural healing abilities and improve overall well-being. It's important to remember that healthcare is not about treating illness, but also about promoting health and preventing disease before it starts. The Seven Pillars can improve our overall health by reducing oxidative stress, reducing free radicals which in turn reduce inflammation, increasing our biological age by increasing telomere length, and reduce our risk of developing many chronic diseases.

Now, you understand the secrets to aging gracefully.

# ACKNOWLEDGMENTS:

Friends become family. Family becomes life times of memories. I would be nowhere without the guidance, love, and support from many of you in the world. I want each of you to know how much I appreciate each and everyone one of you. While I want to write a special thanks to each of you there is not enough time in the day or space on Google docs.

However, there are a couple of family members I must acknowledge because they shaped me into the man I am today.

My brothers Joel, Keith, Sam, and Tommy-from frisbee baseball, backyard soccer games, trips to Texas in the 80's van, to all of us excelling in life. We have experienced life through the good and the bad, but each of you helped me become the man I am today.

My sister Melissa-
Pass the time with you in mind
It's a rather quiet night
Feel the ground against my back
Counting stars against the black
Thinking bout another day
Wishing I was far away
Whether they were dreams or worries
You were there with me

My two sets of parents– Dad and Linda for teaching me to respect everyone no matter where they are from or what they have.

Mom for reminding me of stories long forgotten. And Jim for his knowledge of all things mechanical.

My grandfather, William Mac Luckle, who was one of the last American cowboys. He had a scar on his cheek from bull riding, and a copperhead bite mark on his wrist that he got from reaching into a rabbit hole trying to feed his family. While he never made it out of the 7th grade, he served our Country in WW2 and went on to open up a service station.

He taught me how to fish, rope, and garden. I love and miss him everyday.

Kurt Wickiser was a friend the first day I stood shoulder to shoulder with him as the Lander Team bus drove off without me. I had become injured and couldn't travel with the team.. I'll never forget his words, "My dad can fix you. Why don't you come to Anderson with me tomorrow and I'll make sure of it?" Dr. Wickiser did fix me and encouraged me to have a career in chiropractic. From there our friendship led us to crazy stories fishing in the Florida Keys, to being his big Brother in Kappa Sigma, to telling stories about his 15 uncles who could do it all.

While Kurt went on to his lifelong dream of opening a bbq restaurant, he passed away doing what he loved, helping kids lead better lives. Miss and love you Kurt. I think of sitting on the dock drinking a beer often.

I met Joey Bowers the very first day I got to Lander. He was an Expo leader and everyone loved him. We became fast friends. And that friendship has lasted through 30 plus years. He has literally helped me in every aspect of my life. I slept on his couch in his ATL apartment while I was finding my way in the world. He mentored me through break-ups, interviews, and next life adventures. When I had only a few dollars, he gave me his dress clothes so I would be stylish while finding a career. He has supported me, coached me, and looked out after me all these years. While I don't see him as much as I would like too, I can always reach him by phone and know he will be there for me. He is one of the best.

My current team at West Ashley Wellness. Each of you brings me much joy. I look forward to Mondays knowing the week will be full of fun. Kia you bring the smile, the fun, the welcoming of our community. Everyone loves you as do I. Kelley you bring the knowledge, the research, the serious side when needed. A perfect balance between my wild ideas and what we can do. Thank you for that. Kaylee, I have no words. Except, eat a salad every once in a while. Robyn Rubado, you restore the balance. You are the rock. I love how you work to solve issues. I appreciate you more than you know. Ok. Back to Kaylee. Seriously, you have been a great addition to the team. Your attitude is unmatched and I only tease you out of my wanting you to be the best you can be, always! I appreciate your "willingness". I know your parents are proud. As they should be. Karli, you are the best reel maker ever. I absolutely love creating content with you. Patient, kind, forgiving, caring, loving are just a few of the adjectives to describe you. Jessica B, I am going to miss you as you set the world on fire with nursing. The patients in your future will be lucky to have you.take care of them. I especially appreciate your attention to detail. when working with me on technology things. This book happened because you and I sat together painstakingly making it happen. I could not have done it without you…

I call John Barbour many things: My brother's keeper, my business partner, the closest thing to a man of the cloth, and a man who has a heart as big and wide as his love for Gamecock football. His work ethic is unmatched. He is always there for a call, a zoom, and/or a live PM. Like most of us, he outkicked his coverage in SSB, Sarah Stone Barbour. She is the collagen that holds us together. Love you.

Brian Bilbro has been a lifelong childhood friend. We have sung in Johnny Carson's studios, attended concerts, ball games, and shared the stage in front of thousands of people. I would be remiss not to mention him as being a fearless leader. He shows up first. He is the last to leave practice. He pours passion into people. The only thing he loves more than building businesses is his family. Meredith, or Momma B as most call her is the epitome of beauty, brains, and brawn. Her love of skin care and helping women is unmatched. The only thing she loves more than her passion of helping others is her daughters. I have thoroughly enjoyed watching you raise them to be the confident young women they are destined to become.

And lastly, but certainly not the least, is my wife Jessica Luckle. Jessica was sent to me by God at a time in my life when I needed her most. I had just gotten divorced, going through a healthcare audit, and my life was not exactly how I pictured it. She is the most caring, loving person I have ever met. She runs our medical spa, The Spa West Ashley, like a boss babe. She nurtures our children, sings and dances with them daily. Shows them how to act silly and love one another. And in my eyes, she is the sexiest woman alive. She motivates me to be great. She encourages my wild crazy ideas. She is everything I have ever dreamed of and more. Everything I do, everything I think of,her and everything I want out of life is only with her standing with me. Hand in hand facing the sun looking forward to the future. This book is an accumulation of your belief in me and us.

# BIBLIOGRAPHY

1. Miller, G. E., Chen, E. & Parker, K.J. Psychological stress in childhood and susceptibility to the chronic diseases of aging: moving toward a model of behavioral and biological mechanisms. Psychol. Bull. 137, 959-997 (2011)

2. Fleming, T. P. et al. Origins of lifetime health around the time of conception: causes and consequences. Lancet 391, 1842-1852 (2018)

3. Renz, H. et al. An exposome perspective: early-life events and immune development in a changing world.J. Allergy Clin. Immunol. 140, 24 40 (2017)

4. **WHO (World Health Organization). (2019). "Health in the United States.**

5. GBD 2017 Causes of Death Collaborators. Global, regional, and national age-sex-specific mortality for 282 causes of death in 195 countries and territories, 1980-2017: a systematic analysis for the Global Burden of Disease Study 2017. Lancet 392, 1736-1788 (2018).

6. https://www.nm.org/healthbeat/medical-advances/science-and-research/What-is-Your-Actual-Age

7. "Biological Age Is a Better Health Indicator than the Number of Years You've Lived-Here's How to Measure It." *Yahoo! Finance*, Yahoo!, https://finance.yahoo.com/news/biological-age-better-health-indicator-231144040.html?guccounter=1&guce_referrer=aHR0cHM6Ly93d3cuZ29vZ2xlLmNvbS8&guce_referrer_sig=AQAAAB4udlZbuTZCh7Ty aRiHmxRo3D1klOflcQ8gVm_fbqiu-SPZhELTM4SXy c9NaznxMylTRDfpV7qncxqSJ2qDJHE-GRsOubLpH-8qV-ce8rinbe1BBsaMZVEl9EhX8eVypnviNPmCYAnj aZO8XcRDvLzo51Chk9vPhJRj2MxBefj0.

8. Schmidt AM, Hori O, Brett J, Yan SD, Wautier JL, Stern D. Cellular receptors for advanced glycation end products. Implications for induction of oxidant stress and cellular dysfunction in the pathogenesis of vascular lesions. Arterioscler Thromb. 1994 Oct;14(10):1521-8. doi: 10.1161/01.atv.14.10.1521. PMID: 7918300.

9. Schmidt AM, Hori O, Brett J, Yan SD, Wautier JL, Stern D. Cellular receptors for advanced glycation end products. Implications for induction of oxidant stress and cellular dysfunction in the pathogenesis

of vascular lesions. Arterioscler Thromb. 1994 Oct;14(10):1521-8. doi: 10.1161/01.atv.14.10.1521. PMID: 7918300.

10. Uribarri J, Woodruff S, Goodman S, Cai W, Chen X, Pyzik R, Yong A, Striker GE, Vlassara H. Advanced glycation end products in foods and a practical guide to their reduction in the diet. J Am Diet Assoc. 2010 Jun;110(6):911-16.e12. doi: 10.1016/j.jada.2010.03.018. PMID: 20497781; PMCID: PMC3704564.

11. webteam), www-core (Sanger. "What Is a Telomere?" *@Yourgenome · Science Website*, 21 July 2021, https://www.yourgenome.org/facts/what-is-a-telomere/.

12. Lex K, Maia Gil M, Lopes-Bastos B, Figueira M, Marzullo M, Giannetti K, Carvalho T, Ferreira MG. Telomere shortening produces an inflammatory environment that increases tumor incidence in zebrafish. Proc Natl Acad Sci U S A. 2020 Jun 30;117(26):15066-15074. doi: 10.1073/pnas.1920049117. Epub 2020 Jun 17. PMID: 32554492; PMCID: PMC7334448.

13. Jose SS, Bendickova K, Kepak T, Krenova Z, Fric J. Chronic Inflammation in Immune Aging: Role of Pattern Recognition Receptor

Crosstalk with the Telomere Complex? Front Immunol. 2017 Sep 4;8:1078. doi: 10.3389/ fimmu.2017.01078. PMID: 28928745; PMCID: PMC5591428

14. *Epigenetics and Aging | Science Advances*. https://www.science.org/doi/10.1126/ sciadv.1600584.

15. Cecchini R, Cecchini AL. SARS-CoV-2 infection pathogenesis is related to oxidative stress as a response to aggression. Med Hypotheses. 2020 Oct;143:110102. doi: 10.1016/j. mehy.2020.110102. Epub 2020 Jul 13. PMID: 32721799; PMCID: PMC7357498.

16. ['Mateja Kaja Jezovnik ', 'Pavel Poredos']. "Oxidative Stress and Atherosclerosis." *European Society of Cardiology*, https://www.escardio.org/ Journals/E-Journal-of-Cardiology-Practice/ Volume-6/Oxidative-stress-and-atherosclerosis-Title-Oxidative-stress-and-atheroscleros.

17. Neurodegenerative diseases: Gilgun-Sherki Y, Melamed E, Offen D. Oxidative stress induced-neurodegenerative diseases: the need for antioxidants that penetrate the blood brain barrier. Neuropharmacology. 2001;40(8):959-975. doi:10.1016/s0028-3908(01)00019-3

18. Kulbacka J, Saczko J, Chwiłkowska A. Stres oksydacyjny w procesach uszkodzenia komórek [Oxidative stress in cells damage processes]. Pol Merkur Lekarski. 2009 Jul;27(157):44-7. Polish. PMID: 19650429.

19. Pizzino G, Irrera N, Cucinotta M, Pallio G, Mannino F, Arcoraci V, Squadrito F, Altavilla D, Bitto A. Oxidative Stress: Harms and Benefits for Human Health. Oxid Med Cell Longev. 2017;2017:8416763. doi: 10.1155/2017/8416763. Epub 2017 Jul 27. PMID: 28819546; PMCID: PMC5551541

20. Jiang Y, Rubin L, Peng T, Liu L, Xing X, Lazarovici P, Zheng W. Cytokine storm in COVID-19: from viral infection to immune responses, diagnosis and therapy. Int J Biol Sci. 2022 Jan 1;18(2):459-472. doi: 10.7150/ijbs.59272. PMID: 35002503; PMCID: PMC8741849.

21. Barnes PJ. Nuclear factor-kappa B. Int J Biochem Cell Biol. 1997 Jun;29(6):867-70. doi: 10.1016/s1357-2725(96)00159-8. PMID: 9304801.

22. Lawrence T. The nuclear factor NF-kappaB pathway in inflammation. Cold Spring Harb Perspect Biol. 2009 Dec;1(6):a001651. doi: 10.1101/cshperspect.a001651. Epub 2009 Oct 7. PMID: 20457564; PMCID: PMC2882124

23. Wiertsema SP, van Bergenhenegouwen J, Garssen J, Knippels LMJ. The Interplay between the Gut Microbiome and the Immune System in the Context of Infectious Diseases throughout Life and the Role of Nutrition in Optimizing Treatment Strategies. Nutrients. 2021 Mar 9;13(3):886. doi: 10.3390/nu13030886. PMID: 33803407; PMCID: PMC8001875

24. Barbara, Giovanni MD; Zecchi, Lisa MS; Barbaro, Raffaella PhD; Cremon, Cesare MD; Bellacosa, Lara MD; Marcellini, Marco MD; De Giorgio, Roberto MD, PhD; Corinaldesi, Roberto MD; Stanghellini, Vincenzo MD. Mucosal Permeability and Immune Activation as Potential Therapeutic Targets of Probiotics in Irritable Bowel Syndrome. Journal of Clinical Gastroenterology 46():p S52-S55, October 2012. | DOI: 10.1097/MCG.0b013e318264e918

25. Liu L, Zhu G. Gut-Brain Axis and Mood Disorder. Front Psychiatry. 2018 May 29;9:223. doi: 10.3389/fpsyt.2018.00223. PMID: 29896129; PMCID: PMC5987167

26. "ESR Blood Test (Erythrocyte Sedimentation Rate)." Testing.com, 27 Aug. 2022, https://www.testing.com/tests/erythrocyte-sedimentation-rate-esr/.

27. Ridker PM. C-reactive protein and the prediction of cardiovascular events among those at intermediate risk: moving an inflammatory hypothesis toward consensus. J Am Coll Cardiol. 2007 Mar 6;49(9):2129–38. doi: 10.1016/j.jacc.2007.02.052. PMID: 17367817.

28. "C Reactive Protein (CRP Blood Test)." *Testing.com*, 29 July 2022, https://www.testing.com/tests/c-reactive-protein-crp/.

29. Han E, Fritzer-Szekeres M, Szekeres T, Gehrig T, Gyöngyösi M, Bergler-Klein J. Comparison of High-Sensitivity C-Reactive Protein vs C-reactive Protein for Cardiovascular Risk Prediction in Chronic Cardiac Disease. J Appl Lab Med. 2022 Oct 29;7(6):1259–1271. doi: 10.1093/jalm/jfac069. PMID: 36136302.

30. "Ferritin." *Testing.com*, 13 Jan. 2023, https://www.testing.com/tests/ferritin/.

31. "Microplastics Found in Human Breast Milk for the First Time." *The Guardian*, Guardian News and Media, 7 Oct. 2022, https://www.theguardian.com/environment/2022/oct/07/microplastics-human-breast-milk-first-time.

32. Wang H. A Review of the Effects of Collagen Treatment in Clinical Studies. Polymers (Basel). 2021 Nov 9;13(22):3868. doi: 10.3390/polym13223868. PMID: 34833168; PMCID: PMC8620403

33. Miller, Dr. Mark JS. "Why Are Collagen Supplements like IKEA Furniture?" WHY ARE COLLAGEN SUPPLEMENTS LIKE IKEA FURNITURE?, Biomedical & Nutritional Sleuth Newsletter, 20 Jan. 2022, https://drmarkjsmiller.substack.com/p/why-are-collagen-supplements-like.

34. "Why Is the Bella Grace Collagen the Best Available?" *HELP CENTER*, https://bellagrace.freshdesk.com/support/solutions/articles/73000522388-why-is-the-bella-grace-collagen-the-best-available-.

35. "Does the Source of Collagen Matter?" *HELP CENTER*, https://bellagrace.freshdesk.com/support/solutions/articles/73000522408-does-the-source-of-collagen-matter-.

36. Miller, Dr. Mark JS. "Why Are Collagen Supplements like IKEA Furniture?" *WHY ARE COLLAGEN SUPPLEMENTS LIKE IKEA FURNITURE?*, Biomedical & Nutritional Sleuth Newsletter, 20 Jan. 2022, https://drmarkjsmiller.substack.com/p/why-are-collagen-supplements-like.

37. 37. "Does the Source of Collagen Matter?" HELP CENTER, https://bellagrace.freshdesk.com/support/solutions/articles/73000522408-does-the-source-of-collagen-matter-.

38. **Oral supplementation of specific collagen peptides has beneficial effects on human skin physiology: a double-blind, placebo-controlled study.** Skin Pharmacol Physiol 2014;27(1):47-55. DOI: 10.1159/000351376

39. **Oral supplementation with specific bioactive collagen peptides improves nail growth and reduces symptoms of brittle nails.** *J Cosmet Dermatol. 2017;00:1-7* https://doi.org/10.1111/jocd.12393

40. Khatri M, Naughton RJ, Clifford T, Harper LD, Corr L. The effects of collagen peptide supplementation on body composition, collagen synthesis, and recovery from joint injury and exercise: a systematic review. Amino Acids. 2021 Oct;53(10):1493-1506. doi: 10.1007/s00726-021-03072-x. Epub 2021 Sep 7. PMID: 34491424; PMCID: PMC8521576.

41. Graham MF, Drucker DE, Diegelmann RF, Elson CO. Collagen synthesis by human intestinal smooth muscle cells in culture. Gastroenterology. 1987 Feb;92(2):400-5. doi: 10.1016/0016-5085(87)90134-x. PMID: 3792777.

42. Jnesnadny. "The Heart-Boosting Benefits of Collagen You May Not Be Aware Of." *Better Nutrition*, 31 Jan. 2022, https://www.betternutrition.com/conditions-and-wellness/heart-health/heal-your-heart-with-collagen/.

43. Zdzieblik D, Oesser S, Baumstark MW, Gollhofer A, König D. Collagen peptide supplementation in combination with resistance training improves body composition and increases muscle strength in elderly sarcopenic men: a randomised controlled trial. Br J Nutr. 2015 Oct 28;114(8):1237-45. doi: 10.1017/S0007114515002810. Epub 2015 Sep 10. PMID: 26353786; PMCID: PMC4594048.

44. Michael Schunck 1, Vivian Zague 2, Steffen Oesser 1, Ehrhardt Proksch. **Dietary Supplementation with Specific Collagen Peptides Has a Body Mass Index-Dependent Beneficial Effect on Cellulite Morphology.** J Med Food. 2015 Dec;18(12):1340-8 DOI: 10.1089/jmf.2015.0022

45. 45. Patil AD, Kasabe PJ, Dandge PB. Pharmaceutical and nutraceutical potential of natural bioactive pigment: astaxanthin. Nat Prod Bioprospect. 2022 Jul 7;12(1):25. doi: 10.1007/s13659-022-00347-y. PMID: 35794254; PMCID: PMC9259778

## 46. WHY IS ASTAXANTHIN A PERFECT DIETARY SUPPLEMENT?

Mark JS Miller, PhD, MBA

Kaiviti Consulting, LLC

47. Mashhadi NS, Zakerkish M, Mohammadiasl J, Zarei M, Mohammadshahi M, Haghighizadeh MH. Astaxanthin improves glucose metabolism and reduces blood pressure in patients with type 2 diabetes mellitus. Asia Pac J Clin Nutr. 2018;27(2):341–346. doi: 10.6133/apjcn.052017.11. PMID: 29384321.

48. *How Astareal Astaxanthin Works in Weight Management*, https://www.fujichemical.co.jp/english/newsletter/newsletter_nutra_0808.html#:~:text=Astaxanthin%20reduced%20bodyweight%20increase%20dose%20dependently%20when%20compared,when%20compared%20to%20the%20controlled%20group%20%28Figure%202%29.

49. "Heart Disease Facts." *Centers for Disease Control and Prevention*, Centers for Disease Control and Prevention, 14 Oct. 2022, https://www.cdc.gov/heartdisease/facts.htm#:~:text=Heart%20disease%20is%20the%20leading%20cause%20of%20death,in%202020%E2%80%94that%E2%80%99s%201%20in%20every%205%20deaths.%201%2C2.

50. Hussein G, Goto H, Oda S, Sankawa U, Matsumoto K, Watanabe H. Antihypertensive potential and mechanism of action of astaxanthin: III. Antioxidant and histopathological effects in spontaneously hypertensive rats. Biol Pharm Bull. 2006 Apr;29(4):684-8. doi: 10.1248/bpb.29.684. PMID: 16595899.

51. Krieger, Kim. "Mitochondrial Deterioration Linked to Major Depression in Older Adults." *Medical Xpress – Medical Research Advances and Health News*, Medical Xpress, 7 Feb. 2023,https://medicalxpress.com/news/2023-02-mitochondrial-deterioration-linked-major-depression.html#:~:text=A%20team%20of%20researchers%20from%20several%20institutions%2C%20led,with%20major%20depression%20often%20have%20rapidly%20aging%20mitochondria.

52. Ladislau Rosenberg, Ph.D. "Cat's Claw, a Promising Herbal Medicine with Immunostimulant Effect." *LinkedIn*, https://www.linkedin.com/pulse/cats-claw-promising-herbal-medicine-immunostimulant-rosenberg-phd.

53. Mark JS Miller, PhD. "Managing Inflammation by Harnessing the Power of the Amazon Rainforest." LinkedIn, https://www.linkedin.com/pulse/managing-inflammation-harnessing-power-amazon-mark-js-miller.

54. Sandoval M, Charbonnet RM, Okuhama NN, Roberts J, Krenova Z, Trentacosti AM, Miller MJ. Cat's claw inhibits TNFalpha production and scavenges free radicals: role in cytoprotection. Free Radic Biol Med. 2000 Jul 1;29(1):71-8. doi: 10.1016/s0891-5849(00)00327-0. PMID: 10962207

55. Piscoya J, Rodriguez Z, Bustamante SA, Okuhama NN, Miller MJ, Sandoval M. Efficacy and safety of freeze-dried cat's claw in osteoarthritis of the knee: mechanisms of action of the species Uncaria guianensis. Inflamm Res. 2001 Sep;50(9):442-8. doi: 10.1007/PL00000268. PMID: 11603848.

56. Mammone T, Akesson C, Gan D, Giampapa V, Pero RW. A water soluble extract from Uncaria tomentosa (Cat's Claw) is a potent enhancer of DNA repair in primary organ cultures of human skin. Phytother Res. 2006 Mar;20(3):178-83. doi: 10.1002/ptr.1827. PMID: 16521105.

57. "Chronic Stress Puts Your Health at Risk." *Mayo Clinic*, Mayo Foundation for Medical Education and Research, 8 July 2021, https://www.mayoclinic.org/healthy-lifestyle/stress-management/in-depth/stress/art-20046037.

Made in United States
Troutdale, OR
12/12/2024